A Table of Delight

Feasting with God in the Wilderness

ELIZABETH J. CANHAM

UPPER
ROOM BOOKS®
NASHVILLE

Cover design: TMW Designs
Cover images: desert, Master File; pitcher/oranges, CORBIS
Interior design: PerfecType
First printing: 2004

LIBRARY OF CONGRESS CATALOGING-IN-PUBLICATION DATA
Canham, Elizabeth, 1939-
    A table of delight : feasting with God in the wilderness / by Elizabeth Canham.
        p. cm.
    Includes bibliographical references.
    ISBN 0-8358-9804-0
    1. Spiritual life—Christianity. 2. Solitude—Religious aspects--Christianity. 3. Wilderness (Theology) I. Title.
    BV4501.3.C365 2005
    248.4--dc22   2004025993
            Printed in the United States of America

For pilgrims everywhere,

especially Peter.

May we all walk mindfully

as guests in God's world.

Contents

Preface

We are all travelers! Some of us may never leave home, never collect frequent flyer miles, yet we journey with God day by day, sometimes with great joy and sometimes feeling lonely, hungry, and afraid. Our inner journey of faith takes us through desert places where disappointment and exhaustion threaten to overwhelm us, but we also rest in quiet, green places and find restoration.

The stories of God's people—ancient and contemporary—remind us that pilgrimage is a way of life, and we draw strength from one another as the tales are told again and again. Strangely, even in desolate times we are sustained by remembering the abundant grace of God in our own experience and in the lives of others. God sets a table in the wilderness of our lives and feeds us with the bread of life when we fear that we are far from home and lost to the experience of hope and intimacy with Christ.

At the heart of this book lie the Hebrew and Christian scriptures and two movements derived from them: desert mothers and fathers and Celtic Christians. All were rooted in wilderness experience in which people wrestled with God in rugged places, discerning the divine call to a variety of ministries. Interwoven with these stories are some of my own, shared with the hope that those of us who continue the journey today will find encouragement on the Christian path when demanding times challenge faithfulness. In a culture that deifies instant satisfaction, it is tempting to leave the Christ path. We could take the easy road to the many spirituality supermarkets that offer novel methods for reaching a religious high. We are tempted to avoid attentive presence in the difficult terrain we must sometimes walk as followers of Christ, yet spiritual formation takes place as we learn to trust God in difficult times and as we recall past grace-filled moments.

When we come upon times of spiritual dryness and loss of joy in prayer, we speak of "wilderness experiences." Sometimes the busyness of our lives robs us of a sense of communion with God, or we are plunged into pain and loss that cause a sense of abandonment. We cry out to God, but our prayers echo back to us from the barren rocks of this spiritual desert. *Will I ever get through this challenging part of the journey? Has God forgotten me?* The psalmist asked the same questions: "Has God forgotten to be gracious? Has [God] in anger shut up [God's] compassion?" (Ps. 77:9). Asking the questions is an honest and healing way to deal with experience. God knows exactly where we are and what we are going through and asks us to trust and go on.

Another aspect of wilderness pertains to our discipleship as it did to our forebears'. At various times, those who honored their desire to discern and follow the way of God chose desert places in which to seek clarity of vocation. Jesus prayed and fasted in the wilderness to listen to God, discern his call, and confront the demons of self-will.

Preface

Paul, after his conversion, spent a long period in the desert, where initial enthusiasm for his newfound faith was tested and his future ministry shaped. Early Christians went into the Syrian and Egyptian deserts to live as hermits in radical obedience to the call of Christ. From that movement monastic communities developed to support the life of prayer. Celtic Christians chose isolated places—not always in literal deserts but in inhospitable, rugged landscapes—where they learned to trust deeply in the Creator for all their needs, disciplining mind and body in the pursuit of prayer.

The desert is more than a place of struggle and discipline; it also is the location of holy encounter. Jacob, in flight from home and family, discovered that God was present in the loneliness of the desert. Moses, the fugitive murderer, saw God in a burning bush and was called as a leader and liberator of God's people. Amos, laboring in the wilderness of Judea, experienced Yahweh's voice like the roar of a lion, driving him into the cities to preach against society's inequities. John the Baptist left his wilderness community to call God's people once again to repentance and to prepare the way for the Messiah.

As we hear these stories, God invites us to find our place in the narrative. In flight from his family and from his God, Jacob dreamed in the desert and awoke to the stunning realization: "Surely the LORD is in this place—and I did not know it! . . . How awesome is this place! This is none other than the house of God, and this is the gate of heaven" (Gen. 28:16-17). Like Jacob, we can awaken to the reality that God is in the place of desolation. Like Moses, when past failures haunt us, we can come to realize that we stand on the holy ground of our lives, take off our shoes, and worship God who never left us.

Preface

The rugged shepherd Amos heard his call to care for the poor and oppressed and to challenge power structures as he labored in the mostly barren landscape of Judea. The wilderness where Amos labored provided meager grasses for sheep, and he toiled to make wild figs ripen. This fruit was consumed only by the poor who were unable to buy high-quality produce in the markets. From time to time Amos traveled to Jerusalem with the ripened figs. There he was stunned at the abusive commercial practices of the wealthy. He had no training as a prophet yet felt compelled to cry out for justice and compassion.

In the contemporary deserts of poverty, homelessness, and war, we too are compelled to challenge the power structures that support consumerism and deny the needs of God's *anawim*—the disenfranchised poor for whom the Holy One has special compassion. And like John the Baptist, whose mission was formed in the desert near the Dead Sea, we too must prepare the way for Christ to walk with transforming grace into the lives of our neighbors.

We are the story. The journey continues, and the pilgrim community grows as we support one another by prayerful presence. When others are weary, we carry them until they can walk again. If someone gets lost or is ready to give up, we go looking for that sister or brother. If one moves too fast for the group, we gently suggest that others need time to catch up. Meanwhile, God wears an apron and prepares a feast for us; a table of delight awaits just behind that next outcrop of rock so we will not falter. A song of thanksgiving keeps us moving; a few of us dance, some plod, but we all know our pilgrim way leads to God's heart and hearth, where we belong.

Elizabeth J. Canham

Chapter 1

Wilderness

Therefore, I will now allure her,
   and bring her into the wilderness,
   and speak tenderly to her.
From there I will give her her vineyards,
   and make the Valley of Achor a door of hope.
There she shall respond as in the days of her youth,
   as at the time when she came out of
      the land of Egypt.

—Hosea 2:14-15

Heavily armed soldiers escort our pilgrimage group from the teeming tenements and chaotic streets of Cairo. We leave behind the tomb dwellers who live in ancient cemeteries beneath the asphalt, too poor to afford housing. Spaghetti-like highways soar above human despair, carrying overloaded carts, packed buses, camels, donkeys, and Mercedes cars into the heart of the overpopulated city. I muse on a recent visit to Australia, recalling that the entire population of that land equates with the probable number of

1

Cairo's inhabitants! We pass the pyramids, where busloads of tourists gather and opportunist camel drivers, trinket sellers, and pickpockets assault the unwary. The sphinx gazes dispassionately down at visitors in designer jeans with expensive cameras and at urchins begging for a few coins or, even better, the occasional American dollar. The government, anxious to lure tourists back to Egypt following the fatal assault on visitors in the ancient city of Luxor, provides our escort.

We leave Cairo's urban desert to go deeper into the wilderness where early Christians settled as hermits to engage in spiritual warfare on behalf of the cities and people of their day. The landscape quickly becomes barren. Occasional small farms, shacks, billboards advertising Coca-Cola, and indecipherable road signs emerge through the orange dust thrown up by the pickup truck full of soldiers ahead of us. Our destination is Wadi el-Natrun, where monks of the Coptic and Syrian traditions continue a centuries-old commitment to prayer, hospitality, and asceticism in this dry and rugged desert.

Arriving outside the high walls of the monastery of Saint Bishoi, we pull the bell chain and wait for the porter to admit us and then for another monk to lead us into the icon-filled church, where a service is in progress. We leave our shoes outside and step into the cool, incense-laden interior to listen to the chanted praises of God. Standing on sacred ground, we remember our forebears in the faith who left everything behind to follow God's radical call into the desert. We join in worship with monks who continue an offering of prayer spanning sixteen centuries. The words of the chants are unfamiliar, but we join the intent to lift hearts to God as we hear the call of discipleship afresh.

The monk who addresses us when the service concludes speaks no English, but our Egyptian interpreter, also a Coptic Christian, translates. We learn a lot about the monastery of Saint Bishoi and its fourth-century origins, about the precious artifacts and simple lifestyle of the monks, and about the refuge given to pilgrims throughout the centuries. I am captivated by the eyes of our monk guide as we listen to him. Never before have I seen eyes so filled with pure compassion, joy, honesty, truth, and the sparkling celebration of a person in love with God. I sense that I am looking into the face of Christ, whose arms are open and whose call is clear: "Follow me."

The head covering worn by Coptic monks resembles a child's bonnet embroidered with stars and tied under the chin. The design constantly reminds them of the words of Jesus: "Truly I tell you, whoever does not receive the kingdom of God as a little child will never enter it" (Mark 10:15). The twelve stars represent apostles watching over the community day and night; and, just in case temptation should come from behind, a larger star on the back of the bonnet symbolizes the presence of Christ, always vigilant and protecting those who follow him on the path of discipline.

In the wilderness of Wadi el-Natrun, God invited our reflection on the inner journey of faith. Our hosts had left everything to follow God's call to the desert, where both struggle and holy encounter mark the journey. Why would we, as followers of Christ, choose the way of relinquishment? In a world that proclaims "more is always better" and busyness the means of success, why give priority to prayer, worship, and fellowship with other Christians? We choose this way because we long to receive the promise of joy and fullness of life found in Christ, even though following him sometimes means accepting the desert.

In many ways the life of monks appears anachronistic, yet time with this community challenged me to consider my own willingness to let go of "stuff," including excuses I make for not giving time to prayer. Relinquishment and simplicity were central to the life and teaching of Jesus, and the monastic tradition is the way of Christ lived radically with childlike simplicity. The community of Saint Bishoi offers pilgrims gracious desert hospitality, including grainy home-baked bread and a great kettle of tea. Few people are called to the degree of asceticism lived by monastics, but their lives compel us to consider whether we are ready to invite Christ to be at home in us as we set before him the substance of our lives.

Before we entered the monastic church, we removed our shoes. Like Moses centuries earlier out in the desert, we were aware of the awesome presence of God as we stepped barefoot onto ageless, beautiful carpets. We stood before holy icons that for centuries have enabled pilgrims to see and hear God in the deep places of the heart. The desert not only challenges our inclination to cling to things but also blesses us with the grace of encounter as we walk the sacred ground of our lives. I find it hard to be aware that I am walking on sacred ground when dealing with the noise and crowdedness of cities, the ringing telephone, the demands for attention that characterize daily life. Sometimes I am tempted to cling to blessings received during times apart instead of vigilantly seeking God in the ordinary tasks and times of my life. For almost six years I lived with a small monastic community, and I often yearn for its healthy daily rhythm of prayer, work, study, and recreation. "Let go!" says God. "That was then; this is now. Walk with me on the sacred ground of the present moment, and you will find me in some unexpected places." Retreat time in the desert places must move us beyond nostalgia into ever deepening willingness to trust that God knows the way.

The Wilderness in Scripture

Pilgrimages often lead to a deeper awareness of where we are on our Christian walk. It is a blessing to go where others have lived as faithful disciples of Christ, but unless we also make a commitment to daily spiritual disciplines, we will miss the lessons they learned and the delight they found in God's call. We don't have to travel long distances in order to embrace the pilgrim way. The scriptures and the stories of those who have preceded us also invite us to ponder, recollect, and listen to God's voice. God addressed a question to the first humans in the garden of Eden: "Where are you?" (Gen. 3:9). Of course God knew the answer, but the story suggests that Adam and Eve, hiding in the bushes, no longer understood where they were. They lost their evening strolls with God when they chose a path that led them into a wilderness of fear. Today we can listen to God's questions in scripture as a means of identifying where we are on the journey. "Where are you?" When we know where we are, we have greater clarity about the journey and our relationship with the Creator. Fig leaves are inadequate protection from the eyes of God, who lovingly yet insistently calls us to come out from our hiding places.

Chapter One

The wilderness is familiar terrain to me. My first glimpse of a real desert was from the window of a plane as I flew over the Sahara en route to southern Africa in 1972, but I already knew the inner dry emptiness that those endless miles of sand seemed to represent. I knew what it was to yearn for God, to read scripture and pray but experience only barrenness. I also knew the awesomeness of encountering the holy in the course of ordinary activity, the blessing of silence and solitude, the beauty of tiny things blooming in barren places, and the joyful celebration when an oasis appeared after long days of thirst. This is all part of the desert experience manifested in my own spiritual journeying. That experience connects me to those many forebears whose lives lend me support and who give me insight in the present.

In the desert, a place of holy encounter, we hear God's call. The Hebrew and Christian scriptures make it clear that spiritual formation often takes place in the desert, where stark emptiness strips us of pretense and silence wraps itself around us. In the desert, we find motivations revealed; we relinquish baggage; we receive fresh vision. Jacob, whose lies and deception cost him his family, fled into the wilderness and fell into an exhausted sleep with his head resting on a rock. There he dreamed of a ladder joining heaven and earth, with angels passing up and down its length. When he awoke, he had an overwhelming sense of God's presence: "'Surely the LORD is in this place—and I did not know it!' And he was afraid, and said, 'How awesome is this place! This is none other than the house of God, and this is the gate of heaven'" (Gen. 28:16-17). The rock upon which he had slept became an altar of gratitude as he poured oil onto it in celebration of a new awareness that God traveled with him. The account of the years following his desert dream does not reveal a man changed overnight; rather, we see Jacob struggling and growing until he is ready to return and be reunited with his estranged brother and family.

Moses received the call to lead God's people out of bondage while working as a shepherd in the desert scrubland of Midian. He was a fugitive, a murderer whose hot temper and sense of injustice had caused him to lash out against the oppressors of his people. By this time, Moses had spent years in hiding, and his fiery, youthful vengefulness had been tempered by the hardship of desert life. God apparently saw in this man a potential leader with the gifts to inspire an oppressed people. Moses encountered God in the airless heat of the wilderness where a bush was burning. While it was not unusual to come across a dry thornbush ablaze in the desert, Moses noticed that this bush was not consumed by the fire. He stepped forward to investigate.

A sense of holy presence overwhelmed him, and Moses removed his shoes in symbolic acknowledgment of God's presence. As Moses stood on sacred desert ground, he heard Yahweh's imperative to risk everything in order to lead the captive Hebrews out of Egypt. Like so many of us, Moses put up a strong argument for not doing what God asked of him, but in the end grace overcame resistance. God gave what Moses said he lacked, including an articulate brother to assist in the monumental task ahead. Many of us struggle with responding to God's call, especially when it makes demands for which we feel unprepared, but trust and obedience enable us to walk in company with God on the pilgrim way.

Chapter One

The book of Exodus records the struggles of God's people as they traveled for forty years through the wilderness, and the Psalms provide many insights into their victories and complaints. A series of terrible disasters led to Pharaoh's release of his slave workers. When he changed his mind, the Hebrews had reached the edge of the Red Sea, and he had them trapped between water and the pursuing Egyptian army. God made a way through this seemingly impossible barrier, and the Hebrews' wanderings began with many days of hardship, thirst, hunger, and complaint against Moses. Again and again God acted to deliver them, but all too frequently they forgot these divine interventions in their nostalgic desire for what they had left behind. They did not realize that these struggles were forming them into a community and giving them the strength they would need to overcome opposition and fear.

The Hebrew scriptures are filled with stories of people who dared to trust God with their lives. Elijah spoke out during a time of political unrest and idolatry. Isaiah encountered God in the Temple where a vision of seraphs cried, "Holy, holy, holy is the LORD of hosts" (Isa. 6:3). He was overwhelmed by a sense of inadequacy and shame, but when God asked who would go to speak truth to a wayward people, Isaiah replied, "Here am I; send me!" (Isa. 6:8). Jeremiah suffered greatly and complained loudly as he fulfilled God's prophetic call in dynamic, visual ways. Each of these stories and many others have great relevance for our lives. These forebears lived in the literal desert but encountered a far more difficult desert within as they stood for God in times of faithlessness and oppression. None of them felt worthy, and they all made mistakes, yet they went on. God sustained them in the wilderness, and their stories encourage us when we are tempted to give up or doubt our call.

Bridging the Hebrew and Christian scriptures, John the Baptist came on the scene from the desert terrain near the Dead Sea. It is likely that John observed the extreme asceticism of the Essene community, whose dedication to prayer, fasting, and ethical living marked a sharp contrast to the practices of the religious and secular leaders of his day. This rugged desert dweller made shocking pronouncements and called his contemporaries to baptism as a symbol of their repentance. "When he saw many Pharisees and Sadducees coming for baptism, he said to them, 'You brood of vipers! Who warned you to flee from the wrath to come? Bear fruit worthy of repentance'" (Matt. 3:7-8). The desert has a way of clarifying what really matters and revealing the pretenses and compromises that distance us from the will and way of God.

After his baptism Jesus entered the desert. The evangelist Mark tells us that he was driven by the Spirit into the wilderness, where he fasted and prayed in order to discern God's call to ministry. Jesus felt compelled to spend time alone and to examine his desires, resistances, motivations, and call before beginning his ministry. In that inhospitable place he learned relinquishment, struggled through temptations to self-satisfaction, grandiosity, and compromise, and chose the way of faithful obedience that would shape the rest of his life. Letting go is never easy. It was not easy for Jesus, but he stayed the course and refused the more enticing suggestions of the devil.

The apostle Paul spent time in the Arabian desert, where his newfound commitment to Christ was tested and his choices made clear. In the desert his discipleship was honed and his theology reformed, enabling him to become one of the outstanding leaders of the fledgling church.

Times of solitary soul searching are important for all of us, though our desert may not resemble the harsh landscape where Jesus prayed. Sometimes our desert may just involve turning off the telephone at home in order to be present to God, to wait in silence for the voice that sometimes challenges us and confirms the call to service. A time of retreat, taken away from the usual routines and demands of life, also provides opportunity for deeper reflection and refocusing on God's call and desire for our blessing.

Desert Mothers and Fathers

The desert tradition also found expression in the early years of Christianity, especially in the fourth and fifth centuries when women and men began leaving the cities as a response to the call to love God absolutely. By that time most persecution had ceased; being a Christian was even politically expedient in the Roman Empire. A dilution of the gospel message and loosening of requirements for membership in the church prompted some to pursue a life of extreme simplicity and poverty in the desert. Their choice represented more than an abandonment of civilization, however. Their greatest desire was to leave behind everything in favor of nothing, to abandon this world in which they considered themselves strangers in order to single-mindedly seek the world to come. Some followed the hermit Saint Antony to Lower Egypt, where they embraced a basic rule that he provided. They lived mostly in solitude and stringent asceticism. The cave chosen by Saint Antony when he first became a hermit can be reached today by those willing to make a strenuous hike up a rugged mountain path. From the cave a view of unrelieved rocky barrenness presents itself. The hermit saint was asked how, without copies of the scriptures, he would be able to pray in that place. Pointing to the landscape, Antony replied that the "book" of Creation would become God's love for him. All he needed to know of God would be revealed by his attentive presence to this desert terrain. His biographer, Athanasius of Alexandria, describes Antony, who while "sitting in the mountain had his heart watchful," which allowed "the Lord to show him things afar off."[1] Today at the foot of that mountain, Saint Antony's monastery continues the centuries-long tradition of prayer and hospitality with the addition of a large guesthouse outside the monastery walls.

In Upper Egypt a number of communities developed under the influence of Saint Pachomius, who also provided a simple rule for monastic life. By the time he died in 346 CE, he had founded at least nine monasteries for men and two for women. Small groups of men and women also settled in the Nitrian desert west of the mouth of the Nile in an area sometimes called Scete. Saint Macarius was a spiritual father for many of the hermits who lived alone during the week but gathered at the weekend to celebrate the Eucharist. Today the monks of the large monastery of Saint Macarius have successfully reclaimed much of the desert through irrigation and employ many local men to tend and harvest crops. The current interest in desert monasticism has led to a decision to close the monastery to visitors—especially to those who want to photograph anachronistic monks as part of a tour. But on both occasions when I visited, the monks graciously opened the gates once they knew our purpose was prayer, not curiosity. With its shade trees, glasses of sweet tea, and an invitation to sit enclosed by walls soaked in centuries of prayer, the monastery was a little oasis in a vast burning desert.

The Desert Tradition in Celtic Christianity

The influence of the desert fathers and mothers led Celtic Christians also to seek wilderness places for solitude and prayer. These deserts were not characterized by heat and dryness but by wild, inaccessible landscapes where a life of radical simplicity would be uninterrupted. Saint Ninian, who lived in the early fifth century CE, is regarded as the founder of British monasticism. He was a disciple of Martin of Tours (c. 316–397), who in turn followed Hilary of Poitiers (c. 315–c. 367), who was taught by desert monks. Ninian's monastery in Whithorn, Galloway, at Scotland's southwestern edge, would have been accessible only by sea. It is a windy and wild place, bitterly cold in winter, and an ideal location for hermit monks. The cave in which Ninian is said to have settled can be reached today by hiking across pastureland, along a creek, and over a rocky, wind-torn beach.

Saint Columba (521–597), who founded monasteries in Derry, Durrow, and Moone, left Ireland under dubious circumstances and landed in his coracle (a small boat) on the tiny island of Iona in the Hebrides, possibly first reaching the island of Mull. Iona is a desert of multicolored rock, pounding waves, and fierce storms where today pilgrims must leave their vehicles and cell phones behind. Stepping off the small ferry that plows back and forth from Mull, pilgrims become aware of this island's unique quality. George MacLeod, founder of the contemporary Iona Community, called it a "thin place," where the membrane separating this world from the world to come is almost permeable.

Celtic Christians lived with the certainty that those who had gone before them on the Christian path continued to support living pilgrims. The communion of saints was so real that they spoke some prayers as though Jesus or Mary or Peter were in the room. They prayed about ordinary activities like lighting the fire, bathing, bringing in the harvest, or churning butter—not separating sacred and secular as many of us do today. They lived in the world's "thin places."

From the monastery of Saint Columba, missionary monks were sent throughout southern Scotland and into northern England to spread the Christian gospel. New foundations were also established in isolated places. Saint Aidan (590–651) and later Saint Cuthbert (625–687) became abbots of the monastery on Lindisfarne ("Holy Island"—though not truly an island since a causeway makes it accessible at low tide). The northeastern coast of England, edged by many small islands, is renowned for shipwrecks and also for the wildlife— seals, seabirds, fish, and otters that breed undisturbed in its rough waters. Cuthbert sensed a call to engage in spiritual warfare alone and left the Lindisfarne monastery for the tiny "desert" island of Inner Farne several miles offshore. Here he lived, prayed, and died, with occasional visits from monks when calm waters permitted but mostly with only the wild creatures for company. Otters seemed particularly to have been his friends. A monk who followed the abbot one night observed Cuthbert walking into the ocean, where he stood with arms outstretched in the traditional posture of prayer. When, after many hours, he returned to shore, sea otters gathered around him and dried his body with their fur!

Perhaps the greenest Celtic desert was the one chosen by Saint Kevin (?–618) in the Wicklow Mountains of southeast Ireland. His first hermitage was a cave high up in the rocks beside one of the twin lakes in Glendalough. Known as Saint Kevin's Bed, the cave was not tall enough for him to stand up in, and only a precipitous path led down to the water where he could fish. Later a monastery was built by the river at the southern tip of the lakes, and for a time Kevin had a second hermitage, built on a slab of rock among trees and waterfalls overlooking the settlement.

These Celtic desert seekers were rugged pioneers, driven by their single-minded desire for God into places of solitude where they practiced asceticism and simplicity. They have much to teach us as we struggle with our compulsion for certainty, comfort, and carefully chosen places of worship where compatible social groups surround us. Their deserts taught them to embrace the stranger and to throw a circle of inclusion around those whom they met on their journeys beyond the safety of hermitage or monastery.

The Lure of Grace

In the poignant little book of Hosea, God yearns for unfaithful Israel as the prophet himself longed for the return of his wife, who had prostituted herself. This account of God's grace expresses tenderness, compassion, and a patient, persistent calling to those who had abandoned the covenant.

> When Israel was a child, I loved him,
>   and out of Egypt I called my son.
> The more I called them,
>   the more they went from me; . . .
> Yet it was I who taught Ephraim to walk,
>   I took them up in my arms;
>   but they did not know that I healed them.
> I led them with cords of human kindness,
>   with bands of love.
> I was to them like those
>   who lift infants to their cheeks.
>   I bent down to them and fed them. (Hos. 11:1-4)

The prophecy speaks of judgment and accountability but emphasizes the unending love of God, who will go to extraordinary lengths to woo back the beloved. "Therefore, I will now allure her, / and bring her into the wilderness, / and speak tenderly to her" (Hos. 2:14). When she is stripped of her false lovers and removed from the distractions of a delusional society, then she will realize afresh the unfathomable love and forgiveness of God. She will be reunited with her Creator and Lover, whose sustaining grace abounds most freely in the wilderness places she fears.

Most of us are not called to the radical abandonment of home and family life that drove our forebears into physical deserts where they confronted demonic forces threatening their faith and culture. We may never have set foot in a desert, but most of us have experienced wilderness places along the way of our faith journey, times of solitude when God spoke tenderly to us as well as moments of intense pain and loss that seemed barren. Deserts sometimes come to us unbidden, but the stories of God's wilderness people reveal disciplines and patterns of obedience that form essential elements of discipleship. God invites us to choose the desert and to become intentional about making time for the emptiness and silence in which we leave behind the secular compulsion for self-fulfillment in order to know who and where we are. "The immensity of the desert removes the pretensions of life. The barrenness of the desert prepares the way for the things that can only be accomplished by God," writes John Moses. He goes on to point out that the disciplines of the desert "are designed to set men and women free so that they might see God."[2] Self-discipline and asceticism are never ends in themselves, however, but a gracious means by which we come to participate in God's silence and solitude and to find holy presence deep within our own being.

Some of the early desert hermits did become extreme in their ascetical practices, and the need for a wise guide became clear; they needed an individual or community of other seekers to temper their practices of self-denial. Today the support of others on the journey—a spiritual director or prayer partner—is a gift that keeps us from substituting rigor for wisdom.

When I first discovered the blessing of traditional spiritual retreats, I would scan the British *Church Times* for announcements of weekend offerings in various monastic settings. I had found the desert, the place of silence where like-minded Christians gathered to pray. Happily I had also found a spiritual director who had spent many years as a monastic and had undoubtedly seen many enthusiastic retreatants like me with the tendency to identify retreats with spiritual maturity. My director recognized that I was beginning to substitute retreat going for relaxation and lengthy prayer periods for creativity. Before leaving London for an undirected retreat in a convent, I spoke with my director and asked for guidance on the most appropriate use of the time. "Take a decent novel along," he said. "Forget about being in church all the time; enjoy the country, listen to the birds, play." Though it shocked me at the time, it was fine advice, and the retreat proved to be one of those graced occasions when God helped me to laugh at myself a little and to adopt a more gentle discipline for holy listening.

One of the lengthy historical psalms that outline the vicissitudes of God's traveling people poses a question: "Can God spread a table in the wilderness?" (Ps. 78:19). People had grown tired, faithless, and forgetful of the many times God had provided water, manna, and quail to satisfy hunger and thirst. The vision of hope that inspired the initial group who followed Moses out of Egypt no longer energized a people who had become weary and footsore, doubting God's ability to provide what they needed. The psalm describes people who had forgotten the stories of God's bountiful provision in the wilderness and times when a table had been set in the driest, most difficult places. The Hebrew scriptures repeatedly call upon God's people to remember.

When the present is difficult, we too easily forget past experience of God's bounty, the tables spread with blessing when we were most conscious of our poverty and need. If we choose to remember the grace of God toward us in the past, the present is transformed by hope, and dry places become rich with the soul food for which we long. The gift of memory keeps us on the path. The wilderness of silence and solitude beckons us to discover once again that God loves and yearns for us. We are lured again and again by the Lover of our souls, whose unconditional love always waits to take us back, to forgive all our unfaithfulness. In the desert God speaks tenderly and spreads a table of delight and abundant blessings.

A JOURNAL ENTRY: NOVEMBER 1999—CAIRO

> A pilgrim circle
> Where flies, like desert demons,
> Bug us into prayer.

There is a desert within. I feel empty, with little to give others who now look to me for leadership. I have been reading *Spiritual Economy*, a slim volume written by Father Matta El-Meskeen I picked up at the Monastery of Saint Macarius. He speaks about putting our relationships in order by (a) not indulging our affections in the care of people; (b) setting a limit on malice; and (c) dying to our desire to be glorified by others.

This advice seems apt as I lead this pilgrimage without grasping for gratitude or praise. I remember the words of Cassian, whose influence on desert Christians continues in monastic communities to this day where prayers begin with the cry, "O God, come to my assistance." The incredible poverty in Cairo disturbs me. The poorest of the poor barely survive among the tombs. Father Iranaeus became a powerful icon of Christ today as he pointed, without pride, to his painting of Jesus' baptism in the church of Saint Macarius. On the street a policeman smiled at me, and a beautiful young woman in the mosque caught my eye and smiled. I feel uncomfortable as I contemplate my privileged lifestyle and wonder how I am perceived in Egypt.

I sense that I am being placed in question by this experience. There are many hollow places within, and their emptiness reverberates when they are struck. And there is much clutter like the dust, debris, and filth of this city. I am where I need to be in this wilderness, not avoiding the discomfort or manipulating the moment but seeking the grace to be present to whatever God will show me.

SUGGESTIONS FOR REFLECTION

1. Choose an uncluttered place in your home or outdoors and set aside thirty minutes of uninterrupted solitude (disconnect the telephone if necessary!). Read Isaiah 43:19-21 and savor the text. Invite God to reveal to you those dry places in your life that have been obscured by busyness, fear, or lethargy. Allow silence to be your teacher as you remain open to God's promise of refreshment—rivers in the desert—without demanding immediate satisfaction. What are you thirsty for?

2. In your journal name some of those difficult wilderness experiences that have tested your faith in God. How did God "set a table" to sustain you through those times?

3. The twentieth-century Trappist monk Thomas Merton wrote, "The further I advance into solitude, the more clearly I see the goodness of all things."[3] At the end of the day take time to notice and express gratitude for the goodness shown to you during the past twenty-four hours.

Chapter 2

Pilgrimage

Happy are the people whose strength is in you!
whose hearts are set on the pilgrims' way.
—Psalm 84:4, Book of Common Prayer

The long transatlantic journey ends in Glasgow; we collect bags, then move to the arrivals lounge to meet our fellow pilgrims. We are sleepy but also energized by the prospect of this continuing journey to sacred sites: Iona, Lindisfarne, Durham, Whitby—places blessed by early Celtic Christians whose travels were far more hazardous than ours. Baggage piles up around us, and I muse on how much stuff we carry. Our forebears frequently made their way by sea in fragile, skin-covered coracles or on foot over landscape that was more hospitable to the wild creatures, such as wolves, foxes, goats, large cats, and wild horses. There were few roads, and what those pilgrims owned was carried with them. Now we roll our baggage toward the luxury bus that will take us along the beautiful shore of Loch Lomond, where waterfalls sparkle, tumbling down the green hills. Sheep are safely grazing—

a few unsafely, munching beside the two-lane highway—as the gorse-covered Scottish Highlands unfold before us.

Four hours later we arrive in Oban, unload bags, and embark on a large ferry bound for the island of Mull. In sixty minutes we arrive at Craignure, where we load our bags onto another bus that crosses the island on the single-lane road. We must stop often to allow oncoming vehicles to squeeze by at one of the passing places. Finally we board the small foot-passenger ferry, which plows across churning waters to the little island of Iona. The only vehicles on this island are those owned by farmers and other permanent residents, so we walk up a hill and through the village to our hotel. The owners fill two trucks with the large mound of our luggage on the dock.

We have come as pilgrims to Iona, where Columba founded his monastery in 563 CE. Later, monks were sent from Iona as missionaries to northern England. In 597 CE Pope Gregory the Great chose Augustine, a monk of his own community, to carry the Christian mission to England. When Augustine arrived in Canterbury, he discovered that monks from Iona and other Celtic Christian monasteries already had spread the Christian gospel in the British Isles. Soon we pilgrims will travel on to Lindisfarne, off the northeastern coast of England, where Saint Aidan, an Iona monk, served as the monastery's abbot. The much-revered Saint Cuthbert followed Saint Aidan in that role.

We are on this journey because the stories of Celtic forebears invite us to consider the level of our own faith commitment. We want to pray each day in places that meant so much to them, and we will reflect on the simplicity of their lives, their single-minded obedience to the call of God, and their deep trust in the Creator. We are not tourists, though we travel in relative comfort. We are pilgrims who know that our only true home is God; we have set our hearts on this pilgrim way. The outer journey we are privileged to make is a means by which we journey to the hidden and sometimes hazardous places of our own being, where we confront our inclination to compromise or settle down into comfortable safe havens of our own construction.

Choosing the Pilgrim Way

From earliest times God's people have set out on pilgrimage, often like Sarai and Abram, not knowing where their journey would take them. Pilgrimage is a response to an inner call, a commitment to leave what is known in search of the holy. Some people have traveled the world for many years exploring sacred sites, investigating various religious traditions, and trying to capture the "magic" of a particular place, only to be disappointed. Unless their journey takes them inward, they will fail to find holy presence. Others have not had the resources or desire to stray far from their place of daily service yet have found the greatest treasure of all deep within their own being. They have refused to be bound by expectations, limited by cautious thought, or corralled by dogma and secondhand religious tradition. Their hearts have been set on the pilgrim way of exploration and trust; their lives have borne witness to the grace of God, who sustained them in spiritual wilderness places.

The story of the Exodus reveals a people in transition. They left Egypt gladly, wanting to escape the hardships of forced labor in a land where political violence had replaced the respect enjoyed by their ancestors. All too soon, however, they began to question the wisdom of Moses, who led them into unknown and often hostile territory. They were a disparate group with diverse expectations and levels of faith. The people faced enemies, hunger, thirst, and homelessness as they traveled. They doubted God's presence and purpose for them.

> The whole congregation of the Israelites complained against Moses and Aaron in the wilderness. The Israelites said to them, "If only we had died by the hand of the LORD in the land of Egypt, when we sat by the fleshpots and ate our fill of bread; for you have brought us out into this wilderness to kill this whole assembly with hunger." Then the LORD said to Moses, "I am going to rain bread from heaven for you." (Exod. 16:2-4)

Soon manna and quail became their daily sustenance. When they were thirsty, Moses struck a rock and water poured out. Like other early communities, the Hebrews needed a law code, which was provided when Moses ascended Mount Sinai to receive God's guidance for the unformed community. The people were learning, often with reluctance, to be on pilgrimage. Always the challenge was to keep hope alive as difficulties assailed them. Only when they recognized the source of their strength lay not in comfortable journeys with compatible companions but in the living God did they find the courage to keep moving.

Telling Our Stories

I have been on many pilgrimages to different parts of the globe but have found myself identifying with the people of Israel most closely when inner convictions lead me into dark and difficult places. In my late teens and twenties I was an avid member of an independent fundamentalist church near my hometown in England. We were "Bible based," which meant that we listened to long sermons on the pastor's interpretation of scripture, attended a weekly Bible study, and believed that the Bible was the inerrant Word of God.

I remain deeply grateful for the knowledge and love of scripture I gained in those years, despite the many inconsistencies in our literal interpretation of the Bible. The pastor, who was young and charismatic when I joined the church, became an autocrat as time went by; no one was permitted to question his authority. He gathered around himself a group of men—elders—to ensure that all members adhered strictly to a belief system that drew heavily on the Puritan divines for guidance and John Calvin for theology. Deacons formed a second tier in the leadership, helped prepare others for membership, and served as Sunday school teachers and supporters of the pastor. Women were denied any public leadership or teaching role, but it was necessary to have one or two of them in the diaconate in order to help potential female church members with more delicate issues and questions. At age twenty-two I was deemed so "sound" in this faith system that I was invited to become a "lady deacon"! I was stunned and proud; this role was usually reserved for elderly widows or spinsters!

The pastor was disturbed when I went to college to train as a teacher with a major in religion, a mandatory subject in the British school system. On the one hand he was glad that someone with such a fine grasp on biblical interpretation would be teaching public school, but he was afraid I would be exposed to more ecumenical thinking and questionable biblical criticism. I was. For a time I continued to hold fast to the church's teaching and deny the wisdom of scholarship and reason, but it was a struggle. When I later began studies for a London University degree in theology, the pastor opposed my decision despite the fact that I would be studying in Bible college as an external student of the university. For those of us in the Bible college pursuing divinity degrees, the method of teaching was tortuous. We learned how fundamentalist Christians must interpret scripture and theology and, in contrast, what answers we must give to examiners if we were to gain our degrees. We also began reading theologians who were forbidden in my church, and I found some of them tantalizingly fresh and exciting. I began to feel like a theological schizophrenic, yearning for the freedom of these different interpretations of Christian faith and deeply fearful of leaving the rigid certainty of my own church community. I was in the wilderness.

My wanderings continued for several years. Although I did not give up praying or reading scripture, I no longer felt the assurance of God's presence. The enemies I confronted in this desert included the disapproval of my former church community and loss of friends. I was also assailed by the fear of being wrong, and I lost familiar spiritual landscapes. A subtle voice tempted me to think that by returning to what I had known, I would escape from hunger and thirst. Somehow I knew that going back would be like trying to make bricks without straw. Like the Israelites, I entertained good memories of spiritual delicacies,[1] but memories could never substitute for the day-by-day trust in God to supply what I lacked.

Those who find their strength in God, whether or not they feel the divine Presence, are pilgrims on the faith journey. Trust in the unseen Creator keeps them either on the path or waiting with hope when weariness overcomes them. In the story of Israel's wilderness wanderings, a cloud led the people during the day and a fire by night, symbolizing God's hidden presence ahead of them. Even in times of despair there were those who did not give up. The hope of a few often sustained the frightened travelers, teaching them that they needed one another and that together they would overcome enemies.

I was also blessed by others on the pilgrim way. A good friend training as a nurse in London introduced me to a group of Christians who expressed their joy in God through an unstructured offering of scripture reading, extemporary prayer, and singing in tongues. I went to their gathering with much skepticism. I still believed, as my former pastor had taught, that such charismatic worship was meant only for the infant church at Pentecost and that sound teaching had replaced ecstatic utterances in prayer.

What I experienced was a beautiful blending of voices offering wordless praise to God; they sounded like angels, and their joy helped sustain me on my way. During this wilderness time I also was supported by the wise rector of the parish church I began attending. He encouraged me not to choose escape from this wilderness but to wait for God's time, to be faithful in prayerful commitment to the journey. Others who were given as companions included a colleague who understood, a monk who became my spiritual director, and new friends who also were questing. The writings of Thomas Merton became a wonderful gift for the journey. I now remember that wilderness journey with deep gratitude to God, who was ahead of me and all around me in the friends given to support me along the way.

Navigating Stormy Passages

There are times when our daily pilgrimage becomes barren, when circumstances cause us to doubt the providence of God. During these phases of the journey, it is important to acknowledge where we are and to continue making small acts of trust instead of giving up. It would be a mistake, however, to think of the desert only as difficult terrain and an inevitable unpleasantness on the journey. The desert sometimes issues its own invitation: "Come! Enter into my silence, my uncluttered solitude, my stark beauty, and I will show you depths of your own soul you never knew you had. Come and listen to the Holy One who speaks within, tells you that you are loved, and clarifies your call to service. Come and find strength; let grace encompass you; let go of baggage; and wait simply for God." Throughout the centuries women and men of God have chosen time in the wilderness. Some have literally entered the empty desert barrenness to live in poverty and offer prayer for a troubled world. Others have chosen times of solitude and simplicity at significant thresholds in their lives in order to discern God's purpose and direction. Times of spiritual retreat also provide "desert interludes" in which listening to the Creator takes precedence over all other activities—even the laptop and cell phone!

For many Celtic Christians a passion to share the gospel motivated pilgrimages, and the deserts through which they traveled, though rarely dry, contained all the challenges encountered by Hebrew and Christian forebears. Saint Brendan, sometimes called the Navigator, lived in the west of Ireland from 486 to 578 CE and began his travels shortly after being ordained to the priesthood. Many legends surround his voyages—monsters defeated in churning oceans, miraculous deliverance from hostile islanders, even a ride on the back of a whale! Unembellished accounts of his journeys reveal that Brendan was a man of faith who knew that collaboration with others was essential for pilgrims.

A holy man named Barinthus came to Brendan one day and told him of a visit to an island called the Land of the Promise of the Saints. As Brendan listened, a deep desire began to grow within him to visit this island, but he knew that his yearning must be tested in the community in which he served. Fourteen monks went to a secluded place with Brendan. There he told them: "Beloved brothers, I am asking your advice and help, for my heart and my thoughts are fixed on one single desire, if it be God's desire, and that is to seek the land of which Barinthus told us, the land God has promised to those who come after us. What do you think?"[2] Together they all agreed to go, saying they were ready to face death or life together, but first they must fast for forty days to clearly discern God's will in the matter. At the end of their fast, Brendan received confirmation of the appropriateness of their journey and a vision of the island to which they would travel. The fifteen men journeyed westward in their coracle, first landing on the island of Aran, where Brendan said farewell to Saint Enda, and then continuing due west across the ocean. After about ten days the pilgrims were becalmed, but Brendan advised them to put up the oars and not be afraid since God was their helper and would guide the boat wherever it should go. Finally the company landed on an island where they were welcomed by a holy man and celebrated the Lord's Supper.

For five years Brendan and his monks traveled from island to island, celebrating the liturgical seasons but never finding the Land of the Saints. Much rejoicing followed the voyagers' return to the monastery. Many local people, hearing of Brendan's travels, decided to become Christians. Once again the saint sought advice about his next step, first from Bishop Erc and then from his foster mother, Saint Ita, who told him that the island he sought could not be reached in the small, skin-covered boats he had used. She advised him to build a large boat of timber. This time he was accompanied by not only monks but also craftsmen and smiths who wanted to join him on the adventure. Finally they reached the island and were warmly greeted by the people who marveled with them that the Creator had shown such power and protection in bringing the pilgrims safely to paradise.

Not all pilgrims are pioneers. Most who commit themselves to the Christian faith are, like the first followers of Jesus, ordinary people going about their unspectacular lives but with their hearts set on the Land of Promise. In God's economy when new leaders are called out, some followers risk hazardous journeys while others stay home to take care of the necessary tasks and responsibilities of the community. Yet all are on pilgrimage because all are responding to the invitation to be where God has called them. All are members of the pilgrim community. We tend to record and to hear the stories of those whose exploits and teaching resulted in major movements among God's people. We sometimes forget that they were dependent on the faithful support of other unknown pilgrims. On our journey God gives us many gifts, but the one we most easily forget is our sisters and brothers in all their wonderful diversity and quirkiness.

Strangers and Pilgrims

For six years in the 1980s I lived in a tiny hermitage at a Benedictine monastery in South Carolina. I had moved to the Low Country from New York City and felt quite sure that this must be the Promised Land! I soon learned otherwise. Many people think of monastics as silent, otherworldly people, sheltered from the stresses of modern life and always at peace with one another. I knew enough about these men, one of whom had been my spiritual director for several years, to understand that they struggled with the same problems as anyone else. They too needed to make a living, learn to appreciate differences in personalities, and find ways to deal with conflict. They had various ideas about worship, and while some welcomed the presence of visitors, others were challenged by disturbances in the monastic rhythm. What held them together and enabled them to incorporate me into the daily life? The simple answer is grace, but other tangible realities supported the community. First, they were committed to follow Christ in radical obedience to the gospel. That meant leaving home and family in order to live with other committed people whom they would not necessarily have chosen as friends. Second, they followed an ancient Wisdom Rule written by Saint Benedict in the sixth century CE to enable communities to find balance between work and prayer, solitude and time together, rest and recreation, feasting and fasting. A segment of the Rule was read each morning as a means of reflecting on how God might be inviting the community to continue on pilgrimage together. This community also valued the insight of contemporary psychology and encouraged each monk to maintain friendships outside the monastery and to engage in creative activities, such as art, music, horticulture, and fine cuisine. They also enjoyed good movies.

It was not the Promised Land, but that segment of my journey furnished rich lessons about traveling and trusting the God of history in company with other pilgrims very different from me. The pilgrimage continues, and each day brings fresh challenges as I try to discern God's direction and presence. One essential component of pilgrimage is the commitment to daily prayer and listening to God. This commitment was easier in the monastery since a bell called us together five times a day to chant the psalms, listen to scripture, and celebrate the Eucharist. Now I must create my own schedule and exercise self-discipline if I am to keep it. My day begins at 5:30 AM with a mug of fresh ground coffee, a shower, and some yoga exercises before I begin more formal prayer, which includes reading scripture, reflection, and writing in my journal. In fact I must prepare for the day the night before by honoring bedtime at an early hour, sometimes a real struggle if I am tired and TV pulls me. Needless to say, I do not have a perfect record for keeping this time with God, but the intention to do so is important. It is not realistic for me to offer worship five times a day given the many responsibilities and irregularity of my calendar, but I do return to prayer each evening, and I am trying to pause more frequently during the day to be aware of holy presence. I love the story reported about Susanna Wesley, mother of John and Charles, who, with a household of ten children, was a woman of deep prayer. Asked once how she ever found time to pray in the midst of all the demands of child rearing, she replied, "Oh, whenever there is a quiet moment I just throw my apron up over my head and I am alone with the Lord"!

We do not all have the luxury of early-morning alone time, and nursing mothers may find that an especially difficult time following a night of disturbed sleep. My monastery experience taught me that great advantages derive from having a regular structure for prayer. I continue most days to use the Episcopal Book of Common Prayer, but if the practice becomes simply a rigid pattern, it can turn into recitation of mindless words. The important questions to ask each day are: *Where am I at this moment in my pilgrimage?* and, *How does God invite me to be intentional about prayer?*

Monastic rhythms bring balance into life. Finding that balance is one of the greatest challenges for me now that I have to create my own patterns for journeying faithfully. I have become increasingly aware of how much I collude with the workaholic culture and easily forget the need for recreation and rest. Some of the wilderness patches along the way have resulted from tiredness or mindlessly "doing" without pausing to reflect on why I have given particular activities so much of my time. I miss the monks too, even the ones I was not particularly drawn to; the challenge of life together constantly reminded us that we were brought together by God to sustain one another on pilgrimage.

Today I must identify my community and find others to companion me on the journey. Perhaps even more importantly, I must keep my eyes open for those who come my way unexpectedly through brief encounters along the way of ordinary activities. The disabled man I meet on my daily walk reminds me to be grateful for health; the service person who doesn't give up when a repair takes more time than expected demonstrates patience; the distressed mother whose pregnant daughter has lost her husband teaches me compassion and lifts me out of my self-absorption.

Celtic Christians shared the gospel as they traveled through the countryside. Whenever they met other travelers it was their custom to greet each person with reverence and, after exchanging a greeting, to ask if the stranger were a Christian. When the reply was affirmative, the two prayed and rejoiced together. To those who had not embraced Christianity, these believers offered an invitation to hear the gospel. Many were drawn to the faith through this simple sharing of the Christian message.

On their pilgrimage journey these Celtic believers recognized that excluding others from their company was inappropriate; the gospel imperative was to make room for the stranger along the way. In doing so, they were simply following the ministry of Jesus. After returning from the wilderness where God's call had become clear to him, Jesus gathered a very oddly assorted group of disciples, and together they journeyed to towns and villages, teaching, healing, and offering hope to others. Luke bases his account of the ministry of Jesus around the journey theme, sometimes revealing his lack of geographical detail in the curious meanderings he describes. However, Luke's account does clearly convey that Jesus did not conduct a slick, highly organized campaign for converting the masses but went on a pilgrimage of compassion. By his teaching, Jesus led people onto a risky path that called upon them to travel with trust in the God of pilgrims.

The journey of faith is undertaken with awareness that divine Truth lies in the deepest being of each person created in God's image. Those who trust discover an inner authority that may put them at odds with the dominant religious power structure and culture. The way to stay on the journey is to heed the words Jesus spoke so often, "Follow me," and to explore the personal hidden depths where he is at home.

The author of the epistle to the Hebrews includes a long list of those who lived by faith and accomplished amazing work for God. He reminds us that their eyes were set on the hope of God's future rather than on present difficulties. Like Saint Brendan, these biblical men and women were journeying toward the Land of Promise, and they did so with the knowledge that "they were strangers and pilgrims on the earth" (Heb. 11:13, KJV). Pilgrims do not gather treasures that tarnish, and they avoid being weighed down by possessions.

In her book *Seasons of Your Heart*, Sister Macrina Wiederkehr writes a delightful reflection about the difference between tourists and pilgrims with the subheading "By Their Cameras You Shall Know Them"! She does not denigrate the art of photography but contrasts those who try to capture every experience with a camera to those who can quietly receive the gift of each moment, allowing it to be imprinted on their hearts. She ends the reflection with a poem:

> There is a road
> that runs straight through your heart.
> Walk on it.
>
> To be a pilgrim means
>   to be on the move, slowly
>   to notice your luggage becoming lighter
>   to be seeking for treasures that do not rust
>   to be comfortable with your heart's questions
>   to be moving toward the *holy ground* of *home*
>   with empty hands and bare feet.[3]

Pilgrimage for God's children is about letting go of the safe and the burdensome for the freedom of knowing that dependence on the Creator is enough. Whether we cross oceans and deserts or spend an entire lifetime in one place, Christ always invites us to follow, to open our eyes and recognize him in known companions, in strangers, and in the very depths of our own hearts.

A JOURNAL ENTRY: AUGUST 30, 1999

> Distantly walking
> we deny the deepest truth
> of oneness with Christ.

This morning I read of Peter, who followed Jesus at a distance.

Holy One, that is the best I can do at times, but there is desire in me, a longing for intimacy—and I am afraid. Please hold that desire in the gentle hands that made a universe, touched the sick, and welcomed the sinner. My inclination is to grasp the desire and demand fulfillment; instead, I consent to waiting for your time. Help me to trust myself to your hands and believe that this commitment is what you most desire at the present moment.

I recall Peter's later encounter with Jesus and the questions leading him to speak, shamefully, his own truth. Your grace was held out to him also, and you trusted him with the future of your church. I find hope in the story, and now I find joy in writing.

Thank you for this gift, for my life, for faith that has lodged deep within me over the years. Into your hands I commend my spirit, for you have redeemed me, O Lord, O God of truth. Amen.

SUGGESTIONS FOR REFLECTION

1. Read Ruth 1:1-18. Take time to reflect on Ruth's decision to leave home and travel with her mother-in-law to an unknown land. What qualities do you see in this young woman and her

commitment to Naomi? Reflect on your own life as you name those qualities. When have these same qualities been evident in your response to God's call? Consider where you are on your pilgrimage at this time and who your companions are. Write a prayer expressing your deepest longings and your commitment to stay on the journey.

2. In your journal name some sacred places visited on your pilgrimage. Remember that these may not be distant sites traditionally identified with great saints. Sacred places might include a favorite tree near your childhood home, a friend's kitchen where you've shared experiences of God, a family beach house, or a tiny corner of your own home set aside for prayer.

3. How might you follow the wisdom of Susanna Wesley and claim brief moments for prayer during a busy day?

Chapter 3

Companions

*This is my commandment, that you love one another as I
have loved you.*

—John 15:12

The two large Jeeps groan as they make their way slowly through rock-strewn, pathless desert. Suitcases, sleeping bags, containers of food and water, as well as necessary pots and pans for cooking burden the roof of each vehicle. In addition to the driver, each vehicle carries seven passengers, one sitting up front in the only relatively comfortable seat and the rest huddled knee-to-knee on two wooden benches in the back. I am one of the bench passengers, sweating in the airless heat and entertaining uncharitable thoughts about my fellow travelers. *How come I never get to sit up front? Why does my immediate neighbor never stop talking? When will that long-legged man opposite realize he keeps bumping up against my already bruised knees? Did the person in the corner seat take a bath before she left the hotel this morning?* I begin to wonder, *Do I really want to be on pilgrimage?*

Chapter Three

Later that evening we sit around a small fire in the Sinai desert and eat spaghetti Bolognese prepared for us by our two Arab drivers. We are joined by several Bedouin who had earlier assisted us by finding enough thorny twigs for a fire and by a cat searching for scraps. As we finish the meal and are served tea from a huge kettle, an Irishman in our group begins to recite poetry and explain the constellations to us. There is a joyful incongruity about hearing poems by W. B. Yeats recited in the barren wilderness, so far from the green hills of Ireland. My pilgrim friend from the Emerald Isle had spent many years as a missionary in North Africa and had come to know the night sky from the perspective we now observe. We all share stories, sing songs from Christian and Hebrew traditions, and listen to our Muslim friends as they too sing with accompaniment provided by beating on some of the now-empty containers.

Soon each of us crawls into a sleeping bag on our preselected site—a place with more sand than rock beneath us—and prepare to rest. Above, the great dome of the night sky stretches with stars and planets so bright they seem almost close enough to touch. I am filled with awe, gratitude, and contentment. In the silence, interspersed with an occasional snore or the sound of someone restlessly turning to find a more comfortable spot, I find myself giving thanks for this disparate group of pilgrims, bony knees and all! We are here because we share a common desire to know God more intimately and to follow Christ with renewed faith and commitment.

The Covenant Community

The story of God's vision for humankind unfolds in the Hebrew/Christian scriptures, which record the evolving self-understanding of God's people as a covenant community. At Sinai God communicated to Moses an ethical code to guide the community in their life together. They spent forty years in the wilderness after leaving the oppressive regime that compelled them to work in Egypt. During those long years of wandering, the Hebrew people were gradually formed into a community of faith. Their struggles, disappointments, and bickering challenged the cohesiveness of the group but also drew them together. Later, when their various tribal groups settled as a loose confederation in the Land of Promise, prophetic voices were often raised to urge them to faithfulness. All too often they forgot the covenant and forgot the God of their ancestors.

The two tribes that settled in the south, where David defeated the Jebusites and established his capital in Jerusalem, were often at war with the ten northern tribes, who chose to elect their own leaders. This division of the homeland weakened the Hebrew people, and the Northern Kingdom of Israel was decimated by the cruel Assyrian army for many years until the fall of Samaria in 722–721. The loss of land and identity was interpreted, especially by those in the south, as an inevitable consequence of abandoning the covenant. According to them, God was no longer protecting the breakaway tribes who separated themselves from the descendants of David and from the Temple in Jerusalem.

This history prefigures the many sad divisions within Christianity in which new churches form because differences are allowed to separate us from one another. The hard work of staying together and honoring diversity proves too challenging for many. Bitter recrimination often persists between breakaway groups and those who remain. Both parties think that God is on their side!

The Southern Kingdom, known as Judah, survived until Jerusalem was defeated by the Babylonians in 587 BCE. The people became complacent because they believed their survival signified God's preference. They relied on the Temple in Jerusalem with all its trappings and rituals, but they failed to live in faithfulness to their side of the covenant.

In every generation, and sometimes in our own journeys, God is distanced because we replace worship of the heart with "going through the motions." Jesus quoted the prophet Isaiah when he challenged his contemporaries who had fallen into this trap:

> These people draw near with their mouths
>> and honor me with their lips,
>> while their hearts are far from me,
> and their worship of me is a human
>> commandment learned by rote. (Isa. 29:13)

Abandonment of the covenant led to a painful period of exile for Judah. Although the Babylonians were less barbaric than the Assyrian armies had been in Israel, the displacement of the people was expressed as lament and nostalgia. They were no longer in the place they called home, and since they had identified the God of the covenant with the Temple, they even lost their faith tradition. Psalm 137 poignantly reflects the pain of exile:

By the rivers of Babylon—
    there we sat down and there we wept
    when we remembered Zion.
On the willows there
    we hung up our harps.
For there our captors asked us for songs,
and our tormentors asked for mirth, saying,
    "Sing us one of the songs of Zion!"
How could we sing the LORD'S song in a foreign land?
    (vv. 1-4)

Yet in this painful situation Hebrews rediscovered the covenant and once again found community. Without the Temple and all the trappings of traditional worship, groups came together to worship, not in buildings but in company with one another. Their memories, scriptures, and experience of Yahweh's presence became the transforming element in their life together. The origins of the synagogue (a word that means "to gather or bring together") come from this period. God's covenant community found hope as people came together in small groups to share a common faith; in the place of loss, they discovered just how much they needed one another. The Temple was lost to them, but the God of the covenant was vibrantly present in the gathered community.

In times of crisis we let go of self-interest and reach out to others. Recent history in the United States, when the World Trade Center fell, demonstrates that fact. In that inferno, firefighters, medics, police, and ordinary men and women risked their lives to pull the injured from burning wreckage. In the aftermath of those terrorist attacks on September 11, 2001, citizens who had been strangers found a common bond in their losses and in the patriotic fervor that followed. They discovered they needed one another; economic, ethnic, and racial barriers were broken down in a common purpose of support and alleviation of suffering.

When times of hardship end, we often forget our need for companions, and we may be tempted to form exclusionary cliques of like-minded people. The same danger threatened the people of Israel when they were able to return to their own land. Those who remained behind had intermarried with other displaced people. Prophets like Ezra and Nehemiah encouraged rebuilding Jerusalem but also demanded a separation from "foreigners." Others, whose writings now form part of the Hebrew Bible, emphasized the role of Israel as a "light to the nations" with good news to share. The book of Jonah was probably written at this time to challenge God's people who wanted to close ranks. Unlike most preachers, Jonah did not want to be a success because he did not like the people to whom God sent him. Jonah finally did go to Nineveh, but the story ends with the pouting prophet sitting under a wilting castor-oil bush, resenting God's inclusiveness!

Always God challenges us to ask, *Who is my neighbor?* We are then to act with compassion, justice, and a willingness to learn from those we would not readily identify as companions on the way. By Jesus' time, the Temple had been rebuilt, but in every town or village, communities continued to worship locally and to be taught in the synagogues, though people who could do so traveled to Jerusalem for the great festivals. The Gospels give us glimpses into the various hierarchies that controlled religious life. Sometimes Jesus (and later Paul) used disputes between the Pharisees and the wealthy, elite Sadducees to his own advantage when he was required to answer incriminating questions challenging his authority.

Judaism included many sectarian groups. The discovery of the Dead Sea Scrolls generated important insights into the Essenes, almost certainly the community from which John the Baptist emerged. Like many others seeking a purer form of Judaism, this ascetic, monastic group separated itself from mainstream Judaism and lived by a strict community rule in the desert region of Qumran. We see their traditions replicated in many ways by the desert mothers and fathers as well as Eastern and Western Christian monastics, including the independent Celtic monastic settlements. At their best, all these movements represented a call to faithful service. At the same time, all had to contend with the inclination to close ranks and to deny that others were also bearers of truth.

The Community of Jesus

Undoubtedly Jesus was viewed as yet another upstart cultic leader as he gathered an odd assortment of followers together. He frequently infringed traditional laws in the interest of restoring human dignity and hope. The community that gathered around Jesus, marked by diversity and inclusiveness, exhibited willingness to challenge complacent acceptance of external religious authority.

Luke reminds us that Jesus especially welcomed those who were disenfranchised in that culture—women, children, lepers, tax collectors, and many whose minds or bodies separated them from the worshiping community. Matthew sets the teaching of Jesus into an orderly format both to persuade Jewish people that Jesus fulfilled the scriptures and to provide a memorable condensation of Jesus' words for early Christian communities. And Mark breathlessly records in writing some of the earliest oral tradition relating to Jesus' ministry. In the Gospel of John, however, we find the most definitive teaching about the kind of community Jesus envisaged. The author of the Fourth Gospel devotes chapters 13 through 17 to Jesus' vision of the community that would continue his ministry in the world. These chapters have been described as Jesus' "last will and testament," offered in rabbinic style to the gathered disciples.

This section of John opens with a visual lesson taught by Jesus. Taking a basin of water and a towel, Jesus washes the dusty feet of his disciples to model the essence of a servant community, called together for one another and the world. As he speaks of leaving them, Jesus promises a continuing connection with all that he has been for them. Using the image of himself as a vine and the disciples as branches, he urges them to remain in him in order to receive nourishment and become healthy bearers of abundant fruit.

Jesus encourages further intimacy with himself when he makes it clear he is inviting believers into a relationship that already exists between himself and God, his Father, identified as the Vinegrower. In a land where grapes are a major crop, the disciples are familiar with the arduous but necessary work of fertilizing and pruning to produce a healthy harvest. Jesus tells his disciples that they will experience painful cutting back of unproductive growth in order to strengthen the community. God's loving surgery will make them bold witnesses to the gospel. Jesus will no longer be present among them physically, but, he promises, they will find sustaining energy for their community in the Spirit. The Spirit will come alongside to empower them for ministry. They will not be orphaned, but they will need to move beyond what they have known in order to experience the presence of Christ in fresh ways. The disciples must let go of what has been and embrace with courage the obligations of their future as the servant community of Jesus.

Early Forms of Christian Community

Luke's second volume, the Acts of the Apostles, reveals a wide range of early Christian community experience. The ecstatic joy at Pentecost led to an idealism associated with holding all things in common, followed by disputes about the distribution of resources. Disagreements surfaced about whether Gentiles who embraced the faith should be required to observe Jewish laws. Leadership quarrels broke out, and some of the epistles were written to deal with disputes. In Corinth a failure of love and unity led Paul to write the passage now normative in most Christian communities for the celebration of Holy Communion (1 Cor. 11:23-26).

The church in Corinth, a cosmopolitan group, included wealthy merchants trading in that busy seaport and poorer Christians with few resources and little education. Selfish grasping on the part of wealthy members caused them to despise their poor neighbors who often went hungry: "When you come together as a church, I hear that there are divisions among you. . . . When you come together, it is not really to eat the Lord's supper. For when the time comes to eat, each of you goes ahead with your own supper, and one goes hungry and another becomes drunk. . . . In this matter I do not commend you!" (1 Cor. 11:18, 20-22). As Paul continues to write to this troubled church, he employs a metaphor similar to the vine and the branches. Whether they like it or not, Paul says, they are joined to one another as members of the body of Christ. In chapter 12 he highlights the ludicrous notion that one part of the body does not need another. He promotes diversity as essential for the health and well-being of the whole. The well-known thirteenth chapter follows with its call to love, echoing the teaching and purpose of Jesus for his followers.

Soul Friends for the Journey

Living together as the body of Christ requires intentional, compassionate care for one another. We need the support of companions on this journey, and when we are willing to serve rather than to look for self-satisfaction, the community grows more robust. Squashed in that uncomfortable Jeep, I longed for space, coolness, and comfort and became absorbed by the irritating idiosyncrasies of my companions. By focusing on my own needs, I forgot that others shared the difficult time of wilderness travel and experienced just as much discomfort. It was easier to complain than to give thanks for our common journey. Not until we sat around a fire enjoying spaghetti at our "table in the wilderness" did I begin to realize the gift God had given to us in one another. As we shared stories, our commonality became far more apparent than our differences.

The idealized image of community as a constantly harmonious

gathering of like-minded people does not match the biblical accounts of God's people as they learn to be together. We become companions to one another as we let go of our personal ideals and welcome the new possibilities that open up when we consent to serve.

The desert mothers and fathers chose the inhospitable vastness of the wilderness in order to pray in solitude and silence. Many hermits were also members of communities; few remained totally alone since people came to them seeking support for life in Christ. These wise men and women of prayer served God primarily through intercession, engaging in battle with the forces of evil and serving as spiritual guides.

The conversion of Constantine to the Christian faith ushered in a period of relative peace. Christians were no longer persecuted for their faith, and discipline in the church was less rigorous. During the era of suffering and persecution, Christian believers had met in secret to follow the teaching of Jesus with companions who were deeply committed to the Way of Christ. As Christianity became fashionable, many joined the church. Those who remained faithful and desired help in deepening their prayer went to teachers, often bearing gifts of produce for them. What later became formalized as spiritual direction began with the simple, often pithy sayings that desert mothers and fathers offered to such serious Christian seekers.

Celtic Christians further developed the concept of a soul friend or *anam cara*. We are sometimes unable to discern God's will alone and need a wise guide who encourages us to lead a disciplined spiritual life. Brigid of Kildare once commented that anyone without a soul friend is like a body with no head! Born in the middle of the fifth century CE, she was revered for her generosity to all who came to her in need.

She was honored for her spiritual wisdom even before she became the abbess of a large monastery for men and women. Brigid believed that Christ was at home in the body of every person, and she gladly gave to the poor and acted as *anam cara* within her community. Many qualities exhibited in Brigid's life were akin to those attributed to Mary, the mother of Christ. For this reason Brigid is sometimes known as Mary of the Gael (Mary of the Gaelic people). In keeping with the timelessness characterizing Irish legends, Brigid was present in the stable when Jesus was born and acted as midwife for Mary and nursemaid to Jesus! Inasmuch as Brigid believed Christ dwelt in each person and was served by compassionate generosity, she was, in reality, a midwife and nurturer to all whom she encountered.

In Celtic churches a fire was kept burning continually to represent God's Spirit in the midst of the community. Brigid's monastery flourished for many years, and the flame of her love burned bright for all who came seeking God. In recent years a group of Roman Catholic sisters returned to Kildare. The Protestant church that now stands on the site of Brigid's monastery exhibits stories of the well-loved Irish saint in stained glass. The Brigidine sisters live in a simple row house and offer hospitality and spiritual guidance to all who come. Brigid made no distinctions in her service toward others, and the contemporary community bears witness to ecumenicity in a land torn by religious strife. In their tiny living room chapel, the present community keeps a small flame burning to remind all of God's love and compassion. The sisters carry the warmth of the Spirit of God and Brigid into the local community through care for the needy, by receiving pilgrims, and in the celebration of creativity.

The sisters have inspired others, lay and religious, to use talents in music, art, and poetry as a means of offering contemporary worship in Kildare and beyond. The two Brigidine sisters who reside permanently in Kildare have rekindled the flame of Brigid, and today many laypeople joyfully participate in a community that faithfully reflects the example of companionship lived by the Celtic saint.

Over the years I have been blessed by several different *anam caras* who accompanied me on my pilgrimage. These companions in Christ have offered me the priceless gift of attentive listening, through which I have come to recognize the movements of God's Spirit in my life. My church community, seminary classmates, colleagues in ministry, and the Benedictine monks with whom I lived for six years—all have provided significant opportunities for growth and guidance.

After the monastery closed, I needed to find new companions. As I grieved the loss of that particular community of faith, my spiritual director provided wonderful sustenance during this desert period. I realized, though, that being part of a community challenged and supported me in a powerful way. In my new location, Black Mountain, North Carolina, I began to meet new friends who were committed to their local churches but, like me, longed to be in a smaller community in which to share spiritual journeys. We came together over a period of two years to pray and discern the "shape" of our group. I was interested in the principles embodied in Benedictine spirituality, but others found the monastic model intimidating. We also discovered that our levels of commitment varied with circumstance and denominational obligation. It was clear that we had not yet identified a common covenant, so we decided to remain open to the Spirit for guidance.

During this time of waiting we considered the term *rule of life*. Many Christians use this term for their commitment to spiritual disciplines, but it was not a very appealing phrase to us until we learned that the root meaning for Greek and Latin words translated as *rule* is "trellis." A trellis provides necessary support for the plant but does not determine the direction in which it should go. The plant has freedom to grow and, at the same time, the structure it needs to move in a healthy direction; this was the kind of framework we needed for our companion group.

Members of the group identified six areas of commitment to which each of us would subscribe: stability, conversion, obedience, recreation, stewardship, and action. Over several months we lived and prayed with our personal "trellis." When the group gathered, each person read her or his version of the group covenant. Our individual covenants were placed on the altar and blessed. Companions agreed to meet quarterly. Those who were geographically able to do so gathered more frequently to share a meal and pray. This group continues to provide support for me on my journey. My companions remind me that we need each other not only in crisis situations but when any difficulty arises. We can be there for one another.

In Matthew 18:20 Jesus speaks words that have become familiar to us: "Where two or three are gathered in my name, I am there among them." Disputes among Christians prompted Jesus' words, but the verse has been interpreted to include any occasion on which believers assemble. Sometimes, though, we fail to recognize Christ among us because we are distracted by other concerns. Gathered for worship on Sunday, it is all too easy to be more aware of the chatty couple sitting behind us, the organist who misses a note, the choir-boy whose laces are untied, or the preacher's sermon that goes on too long. Distractions cause us to miss the Christ presence in companions who do not meet our expectations. Talking about our disappointment in God, who seems to have abandoned us, may close our eyes to the reality of the living Christ, who walks with us in others.

Such disappointment enveloped the two disciples on their way to Emmaus after the Crucifixion; they sadly reminisced about losing all their hopes. The stranger who came alongside invited them to share with him the cause of their deep sadness, and then he began to point out the scriptures being fulfilled in the death and resurrection of Jesus. When the journey ended, the two invited the stranger to share a meal with them. At the table the man did what Jesus had so recently done with his friends on the night before he died: "He took bread, blessed and broke it, and gave it to them" (Luke 24:30). Then their eyes were opened! The Jesus they had known in history became the Christ of their faith. With incredible joy they retraced their steps back to Jerusalem to share the good news that Christ was risen.

Christ comes to us hidden in the ordinary garb of our companions. He gives us to one another so that the scales of fear and unbelief may fall from our eyes as we journey together. We share our losses and pain, then find in our dark wilderness that Christ spreads a table before us. Christ feeds us with his own life energy so that we can share good news with others. In our coming together by twos, threes, or more, Christ is present, always repeating his commandment: "Love one another. Just as I have loved you, you also should love one another. By this everyone will know that you are my disciples, if you have love for one another" (John 13:34-35). Love accepts the shortcomings of others and celebrates their gifts. Love confronts with compassion and forgives with generosity. Love stays beside the grieving sister or brother, reaches out to the forgotten pilgrim, and rejoices with the returning penitent. Love searches for the hidden wisdom of the shy and embraces the extrovert's passion. Love binds companions of the risen Christ, and love is the only imperative for sharing the gospel in a fear-filled world. When love widens the circle to gather in all who yearn to belong, the commonwealth of God becomes reality on earth.

A JOURNAL ENTRY: JULY 2002

> They travel footsore
> a disparate, questing group
> who feed on manna.

Our companion group has gathered to begin a time of retreat. Our theme is the wilderness, and I now sit on the screen porch listening to the birds, hearing raindrops fall from shaking leaves and water trickling down a rock. It does not seem much like a wilderness, and yet . . . even in this time with others I experience emptiness and pray, "Maker of burning bushes, help me stay in the arid places until you speak, until you show me the way." In response, God seems to give me haiku images of the wilderness:

The desert blossoms
but few see the fragile blooms
that grow in the night

Arid weariness
parches the soul that resists
this barren landscape

Emptiness invites
relinquishment of safety
from omnipotence

Sounds of sheer silence
mute the incessant chatter
spewed from fearful lips

When the time is right
burning bushes will appear
to thwart waywardness

A fresh encounter
with raw divinity
smashes spineless dreams

"Set my people free"
the imperious summons
into more deserts!

Then the people ask,
"Can God set a table here
in this wilderness?"

I ask God to help me know that the cloud ahead masks divine Presence. I give thanks for the elderly Cherokee woman who sat in her rocking chair after she had told stories to us on Sunday afternoon and remember how her quiet, centered presence contained much waiting. She was but a brief companion-presence, yet her gentle strength "spoke" to me of God's grace in wilderness places.

SUGGESTIONS FOR REFLECTION

1. Read Ephesians 4:1-16, letting the words wash over you. Sit for a few minutes in quietness. Now read the passage a second time, asking God to show you a word or phrase to focus upon as a gift of the Spirit for you today. As you read the same scripture one more time, ask yourself, *What is God inviting me to do or be today? How is God asking me to change?* Write your responses in your journal and add a prayer that summarizes your intention to act upon what you have read.

2. Find some quiet time in which to reflect on your life journey and to name a few of the most significant companions who have traveled with you. What gifts did they give you? What gifts did you share with them? Is there someone who needs to hear of your appreciation for companionship in recent times?

3. If you do not have an *anam cara,* ask God to lead you to a person or spiritual guidance group where you can share your journey in order to find direction and companionship.

Chapter 4
Solitude and Silence

For God alone my soul waits in silence.

—Psalm 62:1

We have traveled many miles along the main highway between Port Elizabeth and Cape Town, South Africa. Finally it is time to rest. Turning off the main road onto an unpaved track, we drive into the bush to a farmhouse with many circular thatched huts where guests may spend a night. After a meal, we each retire to our sleeping quarters, which contain a single bed, a small desk, and an oil lamp. Bathrooms are located outside. Since snakes abound in the region—including the sluggish and deadly puff adder —we are cautioned to tread carefully after dark. We are also alerted to the fact that electricity, provided by a generator, is switched off at 10:00 PM.

I light my oil lamp and read for a short time, listening to the hum of electricity and the sound of bugs beating their wings against the window screen. Soon I extinguish the oil lamp, prepare to sleep, and a few moments later hear the generator stop. My room is now in darkness. Moths and other flying creatures cease battering themselves against the window. Silence surrounds me. I have never before been in a place like this and never before been so aware of the absence of sound.

The year is 1973, and I have left England and seminary for a yearlong adventure in the Southern Hemisphere where I teach at a prestigious high school for white, male students. The boys wear smart uniforms and behave impeccably. I knew about the apartheid policies of South Africa before I left England, but I am ill-prepared for the shock of white privilege and institutionalized oppression of black South Africans. Sleep does not come right away. I am still reeling from the experience of standing in separate lines at the post office, sitting in separate sections of the bus, and knowing that I may not eat with Christian sisters and brothers whose skin color differs from my own. I rest comfortably in my cabin, but the turmoil of thoughts will not cease as I wrestle with the dichotomy between my theological education and the reality in which I now find myself.

Memorized words from Paul's epistle to the Galatians run through my mind: "There is no longer Jew or Greek, there is no longer slave or free, there is no longer male and female; for all of you are one in Christ Jesus" (Gal. 3:28). How can a country practice, in the name of Christianity, a policy euphemistically called "separate but equal," which in reality amounts to the subjugation of many by few? I recall how antislavery advocates in Britain had been ridiculed in the nineteenth century by those who believed God had ordained economic and social divisions. Not only were slaves brought to Britain, but those born to privilege lived in great luxury while their servants worked incredibly long hours for minimal compensation. In my mind, the verse of a hymn, well-known but now mercifully omitted from worship books, repeated itself again and again: "The rich man in his castle, / The poor man at his gate, / God made them high or lowly, / And order'd their estate." The silence around me makes me aware of an inner cacophony of questions and struggles that I have been able to ignore in the busyness of early days in a new land.

Silence is a gift that comes wrapped lovingly by God. There are many layers to be peeled away in order to discover the beauty deep inside the package, and sometimes the inclination to discard a particular layer is powerful. On a night in the South African bush I realized that God was inviting me to persist in untying difficult knots and accepting the outer layer of confusion before I moved on. I was not expected to answer questions that had occupied people and nations throughout history but to search my own heart for truth. Why was I here? How might I respond to the great need I saw around me? What choices might I be asked to make in order to live more compassionately instead of taking for granted the abundance of my white, middle-class status?

Later that night, I again became aware of the quietness surrounding me. This time I noticed gentle sounds coming to me from the darkness. Cicadas offered a nocturnal chorus; unfamiliar night birds and frogs were awake and calling to one another; the wind rustled the tendrils of bougainvillea that trailed over my cabin wall. This was a gracious "silence" through which I became aware of the beauty of the night and its natural rhythms undisturbed by neon lights or radios.

Over the years I have learned to value solitude and silence. Intentional times apart with God in a retreat setting have been important, but I need also to be intentional about creating a space each day for uninterrupted time alone with God. I never know in advance what God will hold out to me. Sometimes it is pure joy to sit quietly and, like the psalmist, to be still and know the blessing of holy presence. At other times, distractions fill my mind, and I need to return to prayer each time I recognize my inattention to God. On occasion I realize that what I identified as a distraction may be God's way of waking me up to issues I have failed to bring into the orbit of my prayer. Many years ago in the South African bush, God gave me the gift of a silence in which the divine voice was heard. Since then the same voice has spoken, often to challenge my complacency, collusion with oppression, and forgetfulness of the call to discipleship. "Wake up!" God seems to say, and I am shaken out of spiritual torpor.

Learning to Listen

During the night, God spoke to the boy Samuel, given to God by his grateful mother, Hannah, after her prayers for a son were answered. Samuel served the priest Eli, who had grown tired, complacent, and almost blind. Perhaps God had given up trying to get the old man's attention so instead addressed Eli's young assistant sleeping near the ark of the covenant. When he heard his name called, Samuel ran to Eli and asked what the priest needed. Eli said he had not called the boy and told him to lie down and rest. Again Samuel heard his name called and ran back to Eli. On the third occasion when this happened,

Eli realized it might be God calling to his apprentice; he instructed the boy to respond by saying, "Speak, LORD, for your servant is listening" (1 Sam. 3:9).

What Samuel heard was not music to his ears! God used the child as a messenger of judgment and called him to a prophetic ministry in Israel, where many had forgotten the obligations of the covenant. In the silence of the night Samuel's life was changed; instead of remaining in the predictable service of the tabernacle, he was thrust into a demanding leadership role among people who had turned their backs on God. Like many of the later prophets of Israel, Samuel needed to address his reluctance to speak the truth God revealed to him.

Prophets are generally regarded as meddlers and not warmly welcomed by those who have grown comfortable with the way things are. In our own silences we sometimes hear God asking us to take a stand on issues of injustice or religiosity devoid of faithfulness to the gospel. Holy listening enables God to act in history, bringing new life to lukewarm communities.

Martin Luther was awakened to abusive practices in the church of his day as he prayed and reflected on scripture. His protests sparked the Reformation. John Wesley begged the Church of England to move beyond its parochial mentality and reach out to those outside its walls. Wesley's commitment to the gospel resulted in his rejection by the Church of England but also made the scriptures far more available to ordinary people. Julian of Norwich chose a life of solitude and silence in her small hermitage or "anchorhold" attached to the church in Norwich, England. She lived through the terrible turmoil of the fourteenth century when bubonic plague killed one-third of the population and the peasants' revolt against wealthy landowners caused carnage. Julian prayed alone, read the scriptures, and knew she must make herself available for spiritual guidance to all who came to the window of her cell to pour out their troubles. She was a listener. Julian listened to God in the scriptures and gave herself to a ministry of listening to others desperate for good news of God's love.

We live in a culture that bombards us with noise. God often asks for our attention, but we tune out the divine voice in the same way we learn not to listen to the other sounds around us. Learning to listen takes place through faithful commitment to times of solitude and silence in which we relinquish our own agendas and let God speak. Perhaps God has been calling to us for some time, but we have not recognized the voice while going about our ordinary tasks. Samuel's response to God is appropriate for us also: "Speak, for your servant is listening." Even in times when we seem to hear nothing, God receives our desire to listen. Often the answer comes in the course of everyday activities or encounters, and we are surprised by grace. God addresses us through our willingness to be still, though not necessarily in the time of stillness. When we intentionally set aside time to listen, we open our hearts to God's word always present beneath the surface noise of our busy lives.

Desert Solitaries

The wilderness strips us of pretense and comfortable superficiality, compelling us to engage our deepest longing for the Lover of our souls. This relinquishment of everything in order to pursue the precipitous path of absolute trust in God drove our desert forebears into wild, isolated places to pray. Many stories of their endurance and wrestling with "demons" of delusion and temptation can instruct us today.

Antony was an Egyptian whose wealthy Christian parents died when he was about eighteen years of age. The family had been faithful in their Christian commitment, and Antony pondered often on the example of the first followers of Jesus who sold their possessions in order to be free of encumbrances and support the poor. When Antony entered church one day shortly after the death of his parents, he heard a sermon based on the words of Jesus to the rich young man: "If you wish to be perfect, go, sell your possessions, and give the money to the poor, and you will have treasure in heaven; then come, follow me" (Matt. 19:21). In that text Antony heard a personal call to obey the words of Jesus and, after making provision for his sister, he sold his inheritance, giving it all to the poor. Once again in church Antony reflected on Jesus' instructions to avoid anxiety about tomorrow and to trust the providence of God for each day. Aware of his need for guidance, Antony left the village and went in search of a holy man who lived as a hermit. With the hermit as his mentor, Antony began a life of strict discipline and prayer, living alone and working to earn enough to buy bread. Any income he received beyond what he needed for this simple diet he immediately gave away to the needy.

Antony's biographer, Athanasius of Alexandria, records the many struggles that the young man endured as a hermit. Memories of his comfortable life at home, concern for his sister, and desire to be glorified by others invaded Antony's thoughts as he tried to pray. Many lurid, lustful images came to entice him, and in his imagination he saw the devil in the form of a lascivious woman tempting him to abandon his life of discipline and prayer. Antony struggled alone and yet with a deep sense of the presence of Christ, to whom he turned constantly for strength against many temptations and desires. In time, word of Antony's sanctity of life spread, prompting many to come to him either for advice or out of curiosity. He then withdrew farther into the wilderness where, for nearly twenty years, he continued training himself in solitude. Others followed his example; many hermitages were established in the mountains, and later a monastery was built. The monks revered Antony and supplied him with bread, but he wanted more solitude and asked for a spade so that he might dig and grow his own small patch of grain. He withdrew even farther to a high mountain cave, and the brothers were permitted to come once a month to bring him olives, grain, and oil. Antony occupied his time reciting the psalms, praying, and weaving baskets.

Saint Paul the Hermit lived on the other side of Antony's mountain, closer to the Red Sea. Once a year the two holy men met near the craggy summit, where they spent their time in prayer and soul friendship. It was said that when they met together a raven would appear, carrying bread to sustain the hermits during their meeting. The close ties between Saint Antony and Saint Paul became legendary. Their relationship is depicted in many art forms, including the famous eighteenth-century icon in the monastery of Saint Antony. They also appear together on ancient Celtic high crosses, confirming their importance to Christians of a later era and offering yet another link between desert hermits and Celtic saints.

Each of these men lived a committed life of solitude and silence. Monastic communities that continue to honor their teaching and lifestyle are active today. The monastery of Saint Paul is much poorer than the contemporary monastery of Saint Antony and located far from any natural water source. Guest quarters are very primitive with no flushing toilets or faucets, although a large Coca-Cola sign invites pilgrims into the rustic snack bar. Water is trucked in each day, and visitors quickly learn the simplicity of desert life in this ancient place of hospitality.

The men and women of the desert encourage us today as we also seek God in silence and solitude. They remind us that struggles with self-will are inevitable for those who follow diligently the way of the crucified Christ. In the wilderness there is warfare, and Christians need to be armored against the many lures of the evil one. The writings of desert and Celtic saints abound with battle images. In solitude and silence, engagement with good and evil is revealed in its stark and unavoidable reality; scripture stresses the importance of appropriate battle dress. Christians in Ephesus were encouraged to "be strong in the Lord and in the strength of his power. Put on the whole armor of God, so that you may be able to stand against the wiles of the devil" (Eph. 6:10-11).

When we choose to be alone in silence, we will frequently find ourselves under siege. We need to keep asking for God's grace to resist all that deflects us from our intention. Something as insignificant as creating a grocery list may tempt us to leave the place of holy listening, but on other occasions we may have to resist unsavory images and desires. God does not ask us to deny our humanity but to live fully and faithfully within the boundaries of Christian morality and relationships. Our strength to be people of faith comes from Christ, who struggled with his own demons in the wilderness and chose God's path for his life and ministry. Jesus did not escape trial because he went into the desert but discovered, through his lengthy time of discipline and holy listening, the strength he would need when he was tempted to avoid the cost of ministry.

Faithful Discipline

Faithfulness in prayer yields far more than ecstatic experiences or exciting revelations. Monks throughout the ages have observed regular times for prayer, mostly in community but in the case of hermits, alone in their cells. The Psalms have formed the bedrock of monastic life, and especially before the advent of books, the Psalter was memorized. Often the prayers seemed dull and repetitious, and on more than one occasion a monk nodded off as the well-worn phrases were chanted. Over time, however, the words became embedded in consciousness and accessible to memory in times of temptation or need. Other scriptures also became familiar as they were read day by day, so the words effected an impact far beyond their initial hearing. I continue to be deeply grateful for the major role given to scripture in the church I attended during my teenage years, and I find today that I can readily recall verses learned long ago.

Sometimes when I read the Bible devotionally, the text does not "speak" to me at that moment. Then I must be steadfast in the obligation to wait for God in silence and trust the Spirit to nudge me when I need to receive the words I have read. Monks are expected to observe the times of prayer or "offices" when they are away from the monastery and circumstances permit. On one occasion a monk I knew began the office of vespers while staying in a private home during a mission trip. Following the opening words, he began to recite the ancient hymn known as the *Phos hilaron*:

> O gracious Light,
> pure brightness of the everliving Father in heaven,
> O Jesus Christ, holy and blessed!
>
> Now as we come to the setting of the sun,
> and our eyes behold the vesper light.
> We sing your praises, O God: Father, Son and Holy Spirit.
>
> You are worthy at all times to be praised by happy voices,
> O Son of God, O Giver of life,
> and to be glorified through all the worlds.[1]

My monk friend did not get beyond the first three words of the hymn. As he addressed Christ, the Light of the world, the monk's mind was enlightened, and he sat in wordless gratitude, unaware of time and place. After some time had elapsed, he recalled that he was partway through the evening office and picked up his prayer book to continue. The purpose of daily devotions is to provide us with a means of listening to God, not to enslave us to a rigid format. This monk realized that he had received from God all he needed for the evening. Laying aside the prayer book, he lifted his heart in thanksgiving and went on with the tasks that awaited him. When God blesses us with divine intimacy, it is appropriate to express gratitude but not to cling to the experience of joy or try to repeat it. The God of grace does not keep a strict timetable of blessing but surprises us with loving presence when we least expect it.

Creative Silence

Celtic Christians went into wilderness places where they could listen to God unencumbered by the demands of a noisy world. Their steadfastness and self-discipline helped them to notice attachments that would have kept them from hearing God's word and following the Christian path.

Hilda of Whitby listened for God through scripture but also heard divine Truth through the men and women she met. Born in 614 CE into a wealthy family, Hilda left secular life to enter a monastery with the hope that one day she would go to Gaul to live as a stranger "for the Lord's sake." Bishop Aidan of Lindisfarne had other plans for Hilda. Aidan recognized Hilda's potential leadership qualities. After she had lived with a small monastic band of companions in the north of England, she was appointed abbess of a large double monastery in Whitby. Hilda developed a strict Rule for her monks and sisters who now lived in the monastery, which was built on a hill overlooking the ocean and battered by the ferocious wind blowing in from the North Sea. The Venerable Bede, who wrote most of the extant history of the Celtic saints, says that all who knew Hilda called her mother, a term of endearment commonly used among the desert Christians for holy women spiritual guides.

Caedmon tended sheep and took care of farm animals on monastic land. During his silent hours, Caedmon would recite scripture he had memorized, turning it into poems and songs. Like many men and women of the era, Caedmon was illiterate, and when there was a feast at the monastery he would slip away before he could be asked to contribute a song. He felt his contributions inadequate as an offering for the educated monks of Hilda's abbey. Hilda heard of Caedmon's gifts and, after listening to him, she encouraged his poetry and songwriting, relieved him of his secular habit, and received him as a monk in the community. From the discipline of silence Caedmon discovered how to praise God in poetry and song. Out of the discipline of silence Hilda grew into a gentle mentor of others' gifts. Her community was enriched because she did not try to control or coerce but to set free the gifts embodied by members of her monastic house.

The monastery at Whitby was chosen as the site for a council in 664 CE to settle questions of authority and polity in the English church. Those who had been influenced by the Roman mission to Canterbury were obedient to the pope and observed a date for Easter that differed from Celtic custom. Other variations between the two traditions included the form of monastic tonsure and the preference of the Celts for simplicity. Roman Christians favored lavish ritual, ecclesiastical garments, spectacular church buildings, and a universal authority that permitted no variations.

Wilfred, representing the Church of Rome, was carried into the council on a litter to reinforce his importance and authority. The Celtic representative, Bishop Colman, had no such pomp. At the end of the council, Rome prevailed. Wilfred argued that Jesus had appointed

Peter as the first leader of the church and his successors, the popes, had in turn received the "keys of the kingdom." Officially Celtic tradition was abolished, though the Celtic Christian love of poetry, music, simplicity, freedom, inclusivity, and diversity has been expressed in many forms throughout the centuries since the Council of Whitby. Hilda was disappointed by the result of the Council but accepted the decisions as God's will. She remained steadfast in her caring role as abbess and in her disciplined life of silence, prayer, and worship.

"For God alone my soul waits in silence." Antony waited silently for God in his mountain cave high in the Sinai desert. Hilda waited in silence far from the place she would have chosen as a site for her monastic cell. We call them saints, but they were ordinary Christians who simply heeded the call to discipleship and followed Christ. Our own path becomes clear through silent waiting with and for God who yearns for us. The cultivation of silence is the means by which we awaken to the interior exchange of love that Meister Eckhart, a thirteenth-century Christian mystic, calls "the kiss of the soul." Our solitude takes us from busyness deep into the heart of God, where we find our true home.

A JOURNAL ENTRY: SEPTEMBER 5, 2000

> Waiting silently
> In the veiled presence of God
> I relinquish fear.

"If you would only keep silent, that would be your wisdom!" (Job 13:5). Job speaks these words to his verbose, "fix-it" friends. He describes them as worthless physicians who whitewash with lies, and Job's experience leads me to pray:

Holy One, show me when my silence is a greater gift than words and deliver me from the arrogance of believing I must "fix" others. Amen.

SUGGESTIONS FOR REFLECTION

1. Read Mark 4:35-41. Spend a few minutes reflecting on this passage and the words of Jesus: "Peace! Be still!" Now practice silence by letting go of thoughts or images. Be gentle with yourself, and each time you notice that your mind has wandered, return to the silence. If you struggle to resist thoughts, you will become frustrated; if you simply let them go, returning each time to silence, you will come to inner quietness. You might find it helpful to "see" your thoughts as clouds in the sky or logs on a fast-flowing river that pass you by each time you notice and let them go. At the end of your prayer time, you may feel that little has been accomplished, but remember God works within you whether you know it or not. As you conclude, offer thanks to God for the giftedness of your life and ask for the grace of holy listening as you go about your daily tasks.

2. In your journal, describe times when you have experienced silence. Perhaps you were punished with silence as a child, or someone in your adult life has given you "the silent treatment." There may also have been times when you thought God was silent in response to your prayers. Naming past difficulties with silence helps us to deal with resistance to silent prayer and to realize that God is the faithful Listener at all times.

3. A mantra is a short line or phrase repeated often to help with focusing. Numerous scripture passages can be used in this way. For instance, Psalm 46:10 works especially well. Try omitting a word or phrase on each repetition for emphasis:

Be still, and know that I am God!

Be still, and know that I am

Be still, and know

Be still

Be

Chapter 5

Landscape

The heavens are telling the glory of God;
and the firmament proclaims [God's] handiwork.

—Psalm 19:1

Heavy rain falls relentlessly as my pilgrim group trudges along the lakeside trail. Mud clings to our boots, making the upward climb over slippery rocks even more hazardous. The thrashing sound of a waterfall precludes conversation until we come at last to a rocky outcrop sheltered by a great oak tree. We pause, looking down into the valley and toward the green mountains now draped with mist and remembering with gratitude the reason for our strenuous hike. On this spot Saint Kevin of Glendalough built a small dwelling overlooking his monastic city and the twin lakes where he had fished and prayed as a hermit. We are silent for a while, catching our breath and marveling at the beauty of a rain-filled landscape. We recall stories about the saint who was in love with God and God's handiwork. Gathered beside the gnarled roots of the ancient

73

oak, we offer song and prayer and are filled with awe at the wonderful work of our Creator.

"Diseart Chaoimhin"—Kevin's Desert—the road sign announced as we made our way from Dublin airport to Glendalough in the Wicklow Mountains of Ireland. This is not the image of desert that most of us have carried with us. It is startling to be immersed in myriad shades of green and to walk over carpets of shamrocks. Yet to Kevin, and to so many of our forebears in the Christian faith, choosing a desert place for prayer meant opting for solitude rather than sand. It also meant a willingness to listen deeply to God through landscape and through the many creatures that share our planet.

One of the most endearing stories of Saint Kevin relates how he prayed with arms outstretched in his small hermitage, probably on the very site where we stood that rainy day. Since the space was so constricted, one arm passed through the small, open window space and was observed by a blackbird looking for a place to build a nest. The blackbird laid her eggs in Kevin's hand, and the saint remained in the same position until all her eggs were hatched! The blackbird of the British Isles is a much loved bird who sings in the rain and has an exquisite voice, not unlike the wood thrush that arrives in my yard every spring. This story about Kevin highlights his deep connectedness with and care for creation, which was a primary source of prayer. On another occasion, when Kevin dropped a precious scripture manuscript in the lake, a friendly otter retrieved it for him, unspoiled!

In the Creation story of Genesis 1, God observes all that has been made and, before taking a rest, pronounces it "good." It is our task as the people of God to so care for the earth that the Creator can continue to look with pleasure on this wonderful world. Attentive presence to our planet and all its creatures can become prayer for us if we take time to see, hear, touch, taste, and smell the richness of creation.

I watch prairie dogs playing together, guarding territory, disappearing into their burrows, and surprising siblings when they emerge from a fresh hole and I smile, give thanks for playfulness, pray for children deprived of space, and sense God's invitation to me to "lighten up."

I hear crows raucously squawking in the trees and love their unabashed demands for attention. These wise and much maligned birds remind me that I sometimes need to squawk and rant at God about personal pain or global suffering instead of whining or pretending that I have endless faith. For eighteen years I was woken each morning by my cat, who sat on my chest, rubbed her nose against mine, and waited for me to stroke her soft fur. She showed me gentleness (the chipmunks may have had a different viewpoint), and her ability to be attentive to each moment led me into a yearning for and discipline of centering prayer.

I taste the sharpness of fresh lemons, the sweetness of honey, the yeasty flavor of newly baked bread and give thanks for the abundance of these things and the diverse gifts of the Creator that give "taste" to my life. I smell freshly dug earth and pungent wood smoke and pray for farmers and for those on our planet whose land has been ravished by greed. I know that my first-world lifestyle contributes to the poverty of others, and I need to reflect deeply on how God calls me to act in light of privilege.

Chapter Five

The Landscape of the Soul

The inner life of the early desert hermits and Celtic Christians was shaped by outer landscape. Those, like Antony, who chose rugged wilderness terrain exhibited a robust faith in which the battle between good and evil was prominent and asceticism sometimes extreme. In the Celtic world, the scarcity of roads meant people often traveled by boat or "coracle." Trust in the Creator enabled these women and men to journey without certainty about destination and to acknowledge holy presence in wind, storm, tree, mountain, and the creatures they encountered. The contemporary Celtic poet-philosopher John O'Donohue names the influence in shaping the spirituality of his home in the west of Ireland.[1] The curvature of mountains, sudden vistas of ocean that surprise and delight the eye, rams in head-to-head battle, wells and waterfalls, all cause him to ponder the mystery of soul. He challenges Christians today to move beyond the "neon light of psychology" and to dwell gently within their own mystery. All too often we try to pound and pull our spirituality into a shape we think it ought to have, but if we pay attention to what surrounds us, we will discover authentic soul life.

One summer I sensed God's invitation to make my annual weeklong retreat in a location where I would not have a monastic community to support me through the daily rhythm of prayers and Eucharist. After a struggle, I also left behind my prayer book and headed for the California mountains near Santa Rosa and the Napa Valley. I was discouraged by staff at the retreat center from renting a car at the airport, and they offered to pick me up. But since I had not visited before and thought I might need to "escape," I ignored their advice. I traveled a long, one-lane gravel road over two mountain ranges seeing no evidence of human habitation, and I began to regret my decision. There was nowhere to turn around and no sign I was on the right track. Finally, however, I reached the retreat center and was shown to a chalet that would be my hermitage for the next seven days.

I intended to dispense with schedules and try to remain open to God's presence in each moment and in the landscape. For me the absence of structure, especially the daily offices of the Book of Common Prayer, was a challenge. I love the prayer book, and structure makes me feel safe, so safe that routine had become a way of avoiding rather than encountering God.

On the first evening of my retreat, I heard a sound on my chalet's deck and gingerly stepped out to investigate. A chocolate brown Labrador had settled down by my door and wagged his tail ecstatically when I went outside. He was still there the next morning and spent each night on my doorstep instead of returning to the retreat director's house where he lived. I asked his owner if I could take him on a walk, and the dog became my companion each day as I hiked in the mountains with red-tailed hawks wheeling overhead. The pungent smell of unfamiliar plants, wide expanses of sky, deer tracks on the dusty path, and once a sudden rainstorm that soaked and refreshed me after hours of climbing over rocks—all this filled me with deep joy. I felt that I was breathing in grace, touching the holy, and hearing an invitation to celebrate the spaciousness of God. The clutter of dutiful routine was cleared away to make room for surprise and wonder at the wild miracle of the Creator's handiwork.

I still love the prayer book and use it daily as a discipline of prayer, but I also try to be open to creativity and observing the landscape of home. Sometimes that will mean watching birds at the feeder, rescuing a bumblebee, or looking at multicolored leaves collected from my yard. Maybe I offer prayer by watering indoor plants, playing with a cat, or recovering childhood delight by letting imagination help me create new landscapes in the sand tray I had made as a prayer tool. But at times I forget and become ensnared in mindless routine once again. God has to wake me up and teach me afresh to pray creation.

In the summer of 2002 I looked out the window of my home at dusk and thought I saw a stray black dog in the yard. As it sensed my presence, the creature stood. I was startled to find myself almost nose-to-nose with a mama bear. We were separated by a pane of glass and a few inches as she attempted to tear down another bird feeder. Three cubs played on the ground beside her where wrought-iron hangers were bent parallel to the ground and clear, plastic seed containers lay emptied and torn. At first I was scared by the proximity of this large animal who stood taller on her hind legs than I do. I made a lot of noise, and the cubs ran up a tree. For some time, they peeked around the trunk, but Mama just hissed at me. I decided to let the bears be and watched with awe as these wild creatures reminded me that God is not tame. Hosea compares God's anger to that of a mother bear robbed of cubs and calls upon the faithless covenant people to turn from their idolatry (Hos. 13:8). I prayed with "my" bear for many days, relinquishing some of the comfortable, safe places of my inner landscape in order to explore wilder depths that scared me.

Landscape in Scripture

The story of humankind begins in the Hebrew scriptures with the image of a garden, a place of delight and plenty. This verdant location, which was God's gift, became a trysting place where Creator and creatures met each evening. They joyfully walked together in conversation until a day when Adam and Eve turned away from God. The pair chose the abundant bushes of the garden as a hiding place because their faithless grasping sowed seeds of distrust in their minds. They were no longer sure that God had their best interests at heart. God came into the landscape of their lives asking a question: "Where are you?" God knew the answer to that question only too well, but Adam and Eve no longer knew who or where they were in relation to their Creator. This story invites us to reflect on ways in which we emulate our ancestors by refusing the parameters of grace. How might we respond to the question: "Where are you?" Naming the "bushes" in which we attempt to hide from exposure is a necessary discipline if we are to live what we claim to believe about God's omniscience and love.

The covenant community that journeyed out of Egypt was made up of many disparate groups whose livelihood depended on such basic needs as water, shelter, and food. Earlier, Abram and Sarai had left the relatively developed Chaldean city of Ur to follow the course of the Fertile Crescent. They traveled northwest beside two great rivers, the Tigris and the Euphrates, then southward along the Mediterranean. These agricultural people knew the landscape well and found within it many metaphors to describe their experience of God. The Psalms especially reveal their awareness of God's presence and sometimes the sense of abandonment by making reference to the contours of the outer journey and its implications for inner life. Without speech, the landscape speaks to them of God's glory (Ps. 19:1-4); God is revealed as the Shepherd who protects, feeds, and satisfies the people's needs (Ps. 23) and as a bird whose wings cover them (Ps. 91:4). The soul's longing for God is compared to a thirsty deer yearning to find brooks (Ps. 42:1); and sometimes the dust seems to be the soul's dwelling (Ps. 119:25). God is revealed as a Rock (Ps. 18:2), manifested by mountains (Ps. 48:1-2), a Rescuer from mud and flood (Ps. 69:1-3), and the Light that illumines the people's path (Ps. 18:28).

The Hebrews were not the only ancient people who found in the landscape images of the Creator and ways to express their experience of the holy. Psalm 104 almost certainly predates the settlement of the covenant community in Israel and was probably based on an ode to Ra, the sun god of the Egyptians. This psalm reveals the ancient worldview in which the earth, like a disk, was supported on pillars between which lay water sources and, at the lowest level, Sheol, the place of the departed. Above the earth the sky formed a dome in which windows allowed rain to fall. The Hebrew liturgists found in this imagery a way to praise the majesty and splendor of the supreme God, who spread out the heavens like a curtain. God's cloak is light;

the clouds a chariot; winds are messengers; and fire, a servant of the Creator. In lyrical fashion the ordering of rivers, springs, grass, grain, trees, birds, and animals is ascribed to the thunderous voice of God who also provides oil, wine, and food for humankind. The poetry of this psalm has the capacity to stir our imagination today and lead us into adoration and awe as we join the ancient chorus in blessing God.

It is instructive to read scripture noting the references to landscape and creation in order to find resonance with our own journey. Perhaps like the prophet Amos, who performed menial tasks in the wilderness where wild beasts were a reality, we have sometimes experienced God's powerful voice like the roar of a lion. Maybe as we look at our church community that seems to have gone sour, we are reminded of Isaiah's image of Israel as a carefully planted, fertilized, and tended vine that has turned wild over the years. No longer does the vine produce sweet winemaking grapes. Do we sometimes doubt God's power, like the messengers who came to Joshua predicting disaster if the people went forward? Earlier servants had returned from their surveillance of the Promised Land with an abundance of fruit. And have we ever, like Ruth, gone out to glean hope from meager resources, only to find that God pours into our lap an abundance that we did not imagine? We do not need to go to the land from which these scriptures emerged to place ourselves in the story of God's redeeming, grace-filled work. We can look out the window, listen to the miracle of our own heartbeat, watch dust motes floating in a sunbeam, or listen to the sound of birds and know that God is alive and well in this world of daily miracles.

Chapter Five

Jesus and Nature

Jesus observed the landscape, and his teaching reflected the wisdom of paying attention to nature as a source of confidence in God's provision. "Do not worry about your life . . . ," Jesus said. "Look at the birds of the air; they neither reap nor gather into barns, and yet your heavenly Father feeds them. Are you not of more value than they? . . . And why do you worry about clothing? Consider the lilies of the field, how they grow; they neither toil nor spin, yet I tell you, even Solomon in all his glory was not clothed like one of these. But if God so clothes the grass of the field, which is alive today and tomorrow is thrown into the oven, will [God] not much more clothe you?" (Matt. 6:25-30).

In the parable of the sower, seed is a metaphor for the way in which God's word is received or lost (Matt. 13:1-23). Sometimes the seed of the word falls on frequently trodden pathways and is snatched away by birds of forgetfulness. Seed may also land in rocky places but, after an initial burst of enthusiasm, it begins to die because there it cannot endure hard times. Other seed lands where it must compete with the thorny barbs of worry and wealth, which, all too soon, choke it. But some seed finds its way into soil that has been fertilized and well prepared; this seed grows into a healthy harvest. In each of us, all four locations exist, and Jesus calls upon us to tend the soil of our lives so that we may become fruitful bearers of good news to the world.

Jesus was faithful to his Jewish tradition, honoring the sabbath and worshiping with his community in the synagogue. He also chose places in nature where he could be alone to pray. The predawn darkness of a deserted place provided respite in the midst of a busy and demanding ministry (Mark 1:35). Jesus prayed in the temple and synagogue but was often drawn into the unpeopled wilderness. John makes reference to Jesus going to a mountain alone to escape the adulation of the crowd, following the feeding of the five thousand. Jesus had rejected the temptation to seize popularity during his forty-day pre-ministry retreat in the desert, but he faced this temptation again after he fed a great crowd. The disciples rowed out into the lake where a fierce windstorm threatened their safety until Jesus joined them.

Celtic Christians, who ventured into the unknown trusting the Creator to protect them, loved this story. Alexander Carmichael (1832–1912) collected many of their prayers and blessings as he traveled the Highlands and islands of the Celtic world in the capacity of an excise officer. The prayers were transmitted orally over many centuries and remained vibrant among shepherds, farmers, and fishermen who encountered the elements daily in these often inhospitable landscapes and seascapes.

> God be with thee in every pass,
> Jesus be with thee on every hill,
> Spirit be with thee on every stream,
> Headland and ridge and lawn;
>
> Each sea and land, each moor and meadow,
> Each lying down, each rising up,
> In the trough of the waves, on the crest of the billows,
> Each step of the journey thou goest.[2]

Unlettered people of the Celtic world transmitted Gospel stories through the many intricately carved high crosses. The crosses, scattered throughout the countryside in the British Isles, were probably outdoor gathering places where Christians prayed together. Scenes from the life, teaching, and crucifixion of Jesus are intertwined with vines, birds, and animal figures on these crosses. Monks who executed detailed illuminated manuscript copies of the scriptures placed many creatures in their work, including wonderfully fantastic birds and animals. The monastics took their faith seriously but also honored creativity and humor. Perhaps the cat at one corner of a page and the mouse hiding in Celtic knot-work at another were inspired by images Jesus presented, such as a camel trying to pass through a needle's eye and a person with a great log in the eye trying to remove a tiny splinter from someone else's eye!

Landscape and Creativity

Outer and inner landscape come together in creativity. Much of the world's poetry is inspired by landscape, and an art gallery can become a place of prayer as the viewer stands before beauty or pain depicted in a painting. Artists, musicians, writers, filmmakers, and craftspeople inspire us to see the world and human experience in fresh ways. They also may stir within us a desire to express our own creativity in surprising ways once we get beyond the fear of "coloring outside the lines"! Many people deny having any creative gifts. But we are made in the image of the Creator, who continues to bring beauty to light through us.

A friend of mine begins her daily prayer time with a sketchbook and box of crayons, either drawing dream images or simply using color to express feeling. She is unlikely to see any of her work hung in the Metropolitan Museum of Art, but the act of creative expression puts her in touch with her inner landscape and provides a focus for prayer. A well-educated woman with theological training, my friend recognizes that words and study actually can prevent her from hearing God's invitation in the present moment.

A man whose home incorporates wood fires for central heating and hot water finds that his best prayer time occurs in the yard while he splits logs. He honors the trees that now provide fuel. Each day he walks over rutted fields with his dogs, listening to the warning cries of pheasants, watches deer grazing, and celebrates the dawn—gift of a new day. This is prayer, offered in the windy, rainy climate of England and acknowledging the Mystery at the heart of all creation.

God invites each one of us to be prayerfully present to the created world and to the inner landscape of our souls so often reflected in it. Whether we see the beauty of a sunset or smell the stench of manure, prayer can become real. The sunset may invoke awe at the magnificent beauty of all the Creator made, including the intricate weaving of our own souls, or it may be a reminder to number our days and live wisely (Ps. 90:12). Manure may reflect ways in which we turn away from unpleasant things that need our attention, or it may be a metaphor for the grace by which God redeems our old habits and choices in order to fertilize new life now growing within. And our four-legged, feathered, finned, and scaly friends will also teach us to pray if we let them.

Chapter Five

The silly goose
went to a cold place
and is now rooted, stuck fast in
ice.
Isolated
on a brittle floe,
she is struggling to escape
as rescuers draw near.
She cannot free herself
yet resists help,
while distant companions
feed together in buoyant water.
Release!
Will the goose remember
that ice is not recommended
for meditation?

This morning I began my walk around Lake Tomahawk by watching a goose rescue. A crowd had gathered, and two young boys in a rowboat made their way slowly toward the bird, smashing ice as they went. Rowing was not possible, so they used a pole to punt forward until finally enough ice was broken and the goose was free. Does God see me sometimes as a *silly goose*? I recall the term used in childhood, usually with compassion and affection.

Holy One, help me to laugh at myself when I get stuck in odd places because I am not paying attention to where you are leading me. Thank you for the goose who reminds me not to resist your approach. And thank you for the unpredictability of your Spirit, so often represented by Celtic Christians as the wild goose who will not be tamed. Amen.

SUGGESTIONS FOR REFLECTION

1. Read Psalm 104 and allow your imagination to focus on the images of God and the unfolding mystery of creation celebrated in this song. Sit quietly and recall experiences of being in nature and interacting with other creatures; jot down these memories. Return to the psalm and use its structure as a model but rewrite it, naming your remembered moments of presence in the natural world. When you have finished, say your psalm slowly as a prayer of gratitude.

2. Choose a natural object—a stone, feather, pinecone, leaf—and hold it gently. Spend a few moments simply observing the object, noticing color, shape, and texture. Now allow your mind to wander to any memory, image, experience, or scripture verse the object suggests to you. Finally, choose one of these reflections as a focus and continue to allow its "energy" to become your prayer.

3. Become intentional about observing the phases of the moon and the rhythm of days, months, and seasons. Offer the following sevenfold prayer adapted from sevenfold prayers in the Celtic and Native American traditions. If possible, stand outside, allowing your body to pray the simple movements:

- Face east, extending your hand toward the place of sunrise and say: *Light of the World, illumine our darkness and bless with hope all who come from the east. Amen.*

- Face south, extending your hand as you recall noonday and say: *Fire in Our Hearts, kindle compassion and awaken joy in all who come from the south. Amen.*

- Face west, extending your hand toward the place of the setting sun and say: *Sabbath Giver, may we remember all who toil as we rest in your peace. Amen.*

- Face north, extending your hand as you recall midnight darkness and say: *Creator of Moon and Stars, bless all who are afraid and grant us healing dreams. Amen.*

- Extend your hand or bow to the earth and say: *Word Made Flesh, teach us to work with you to share the harvest of good with all your creatures. Amen.*

- Lift both hands upward and say: *All-loving Creator, fill our lives with gratitude and bring all people into the circle of your enfolding grace. Amen.*

- Place your hand on your heart and say: *Indwelling Spirit, awaken us to your life lived in our humanity and bless all whose hearts are aching for your presence. Amen.*

Chapter 6

Wells

[Jesus] came to a Samaritan city called Sychar, near the plot of ground that Jacob had given to his son Joseph. Jacob's well was there, and Jesus, tired out by his journey, was sitting by the well. It was about noon.

—John 4:5-6

The small Welsh town of Saint David's, named for the patron saint of Wales, overlooks the ocean and a craggy peninsula. We pilgrims come to this place in the season of wildflowers and honeysuckle, and of course we visit the cathedral where David is buried; its cool interior welcomes us after the unusually warm days we have enjoyed. For many of us, however, the tiny ruined church in a cow pasture and a well at the entrance draw us even more deeply into a sense of mystery and holy presence. We linger to hear the story of Non, mother of David, and to reflect on her role as a woman of courage who knew Christ, the source of living water, symbolized in the well dedicated to her. Non was a woman of royal lineage, a devout Christian, who was raped by King Sanctus. She continued to live a devout life of prayer and fasting as she carried her child to term. Alone on the clifftop during a wild storm, Non went into labor and gave birth to David in about 460 CE. Around her, wind, rain, thunder, and lightning raged, but, according to tradition, she was encircled by holy light and peaceful calm.

Pure water flows in Saint Non's well, and we gather around to share generous cupfuls and to refresh our faces with its coolness. We also recall our baptism into Christ, expressing gratitude for the faith of our forebears whose discipleship carried the gospel into Celtic lands. Watched by curious cattle, we walk into the pasture and gather in the tiny ruin of Saint Non's church to celebrate the Eucharist together, using one of the rough rocks as an altar. An ancient standing stone, marked by what could be seen as handprints, is said to be the place where Non gripped for support as her labor progressed. We do not try to separate myth from history but sense the sacredness of this ancient site and celebrate the life of David's mother and her deep trust in God.

We read the story of Jesus' encounter with the Samaritan woman at the well in Sychar and talk together of the thirst we bring on this pilgrimage. Jesus broke through many barriers when he made himself available to the woman whose life was arid, though she had tried to satisfy longing with sexual encounters. Jesus stepped out of gender, religious, and social conventions in order to invite her service and interest. The well became a visible metaphor used by Jesus to speak to her of the fullness of life he embodied. She experienced transformation. Now the woman could not wait to tell the villagers she had formerly attempted to avoid by coming to the well in the heat of the day: "Come and see a man who told me everything I have ever done! He cannot be the Messiah, can he?" (John 4:29). Many came, asked Jesus to stay and teach them. Samaritans, despised by Jewish tradition, received the gospel.

Our group begins to share stories of thirsty times in our lives, times when God seemed absent and prayer became brittle and dry. Often our wilderness experiences followed a time of loss when we wondered if we would ever recover the experience of God's presence, only to be surprised by grace. Sometimes we had become too busy to make space for God, and sometimes our lives were caught up in empty pleasure seeking or a relationship that had grown stale. Again and again God lovingly beckoned us back and led us to the only source of abundant, refreshing life in Christ.

We also became aware that in human experience, dry places are inevitable no matter how faithfully we observe spiritual disciplines. We can learn deep lessons of trust and transformation in the spiritual desert. Many of those whom we now call saints testify to long periods of drought in their prayer. Their experience encourages us to regard God not as a bully but as a gracious disciplinarian who knows we grow through struggle and loss of cozy feelings.

Following a long list of people of faith and an encouragement for readers to emulate a great "cloud of witnesses," the author of the epistle to the Hebrews writes: "Now, discipline always seems painful rather than pleasant at the time, but later it yields the peaceful fruit of righteousness to those who have been trained by it" (Heb. 12:11). It was a blessing to many of us to realize that when our Shepherd-God did not lead us to still waters right away, we learned important lessons. We walked the valley of the shadow of death and discovered utter faithfulness of the One to whom we prayed without reward. God prepared a table for us even in the wilderness place where the enemies of fear, ridicule, anger, helplessness, and misunderstanding threatened us, and our souls were restored to hope (Ps. 23).

Wilderness Wells

Among the Hebrews, water sources determined the course of travel and settlement. When Abram and Sarai left Ur, a city located about two hundred miles south of present-day Baghdad, they traveled northwest through Iraq following the course of the two great rivers, Tigris and Euphrates, a route that became known as the Fertile Crescent. Traders followed this course for many centuries, turning south along the Mediterranean through present-day Israel, also rich in fertile land. Abram's first settlement was in Haran beside a tributary of the Euphrates, the river Balikh. His company then continued southward into Egypt with their flocks and herds.

A critical moment arrived when they returned through Israel and settled with their expanded families and animals near Bethel. It was clear that the land could not support the expanding families of Lot and Abram. Abram allowed Lot to choose his location to avoid strife between their respective herders and families, and Lot predictably chose the richest land. As these early forebears of our faith settled the land, they dug wells to supply the needs of their tented communities and the sheep, goats, and cattle that represented their wealth.

Hebrew scriptures contain many references to wells. Wells often became associated with the patriarch whose family settled an area, sometimes ousting others from desirable land suitable for pasture. Wells were essential to sustain life in the wilderness, so it is not surprising that wells became a metaphor for God's sustaining grace and rescue from disaster. "With joy you will draw water from the wells of salvation" (Isa. 12:3). A pilgrim psalm celebrates not only physical desolation and refreshment but the inner change that takes place for those traveling with trust:

> Happy are the people whose strength is in you!
>> whose hearts are set on the pilgrims' way.
> Those who go through the desolate valley will find
>> it a place of springs (wells). (Ps. 84:4-5, Book of
>> Common Prayer)

Wells were protected, venerated, and they became meeting places where people (mostly women) would gather to draw water and share stories. The mention of wells reminds us to ask, *What am I thirsting for at this time?*

God's words are compared to abundant water by the author we have come to call Second Isaiah. All are invited to come and to be refreshed:

> Ho, everyone who thirsts, come to the waters;
> and you that have no money, come, buy and eat!
> Come, buy wine and milk without money and without
>> price. (Isa. 55:1)

Repeatedly in this passage God asks us to listen, to "incline our ears," and promises that the word will come to fruition:

93

For as the rain and the snow come down from heaven,
 and do not return there until they have watered
  the earth,
making it bring forth and sprout,
 giving seed to the sower and bread to the eater,
so shall my word be that goes out from my mouth;
 it shall not return to me empty. (Isa. 55:10-11)

God offers generous promises to those who will pay attention and create time in their lives for listening deeply to the divine voice. That voice calls them to a life of discipline, gratitude, and reflection on the Word. Others miss those promises when they fall asleep and expect God to become a kind of itinerant water carrier. Happily, God also has a way of making us so thirsty in our forgetfulness that we are compelled to return again to the only source of true, satisfying refreshment.

Filling wells with debris was one of the most devastating things an enemy could do to a community, thus cutting off the source of life. Laboriously unblocking the well, digging deep enough to relocate the hidden water supply, was necessary for the community to survive. Sometimes our spiritual experience resembles a blocked well, and we face the task of clearing out the rubble of fear, pride, and conditioning that prevents our drinking deeply of Christ.

I grew up in an old house that had once served as an inn, with overnight accommodations for both travelers and the horses that pulled stagecoaches between London and the north of England. A long yard with stables at the end (used as a henhouse and garages when we lived there) made an ideal playground for my siblings and me. Halfway down the yard was a large concrete slab, which we were forbidden to use for our games; it covered an ancient well, and my mother feared its collapse. Many years later, when the house was demolished to make way for a new shopping center, earthmoving equipment uncovered the well and found that it was indeed deep, requiring some twenty truckloads of "filler."

I had forgotten that well until, as I led a retreat for women, we reflected together on the story of Jesus and the Samaritan woman at Jacob's well. We began to talk of the blocks we had experienced in our families, jobs, churches, and education, leading many of us to feelings of inadequacy and self-criticism. Some had abandoned churches where they were treated as second-class; others had left abusive marriages; still others had simply accepted a role as nice, compliant, selfless caregivers who continued to attend places of worship where they were marginalized by the language and leadership. We began to see ourselves as wells that were blocked! A lively discussion took place as we looked at ways to remove the "concrete slabs" that kept us from drinking deeply from the life of Christ within.

In his encounter with the woman at the well, Jesus did not offer a new program; nor did he begin with a criticism of her lifestyle. Instead he helped her to realize that the thirst she had tried to quench by reaching outside herself would be slaked only if she chose to go within to discover the Christ presence. Her reputation, experiences of rejection, and disenfranchisement as a woman in a patriarchal culture were part of the concrete mix that blocked the life-giving water of Christ. Jesus, by his compassionate acceptance of her as she was, helped her to lift that heavy burden. She was transformed by holy joy as she tapped the thirst-quenching essence of her being. "Those who drink of the water that I will give them will never be thirsty. The water that I will give will become in them a spring of water gushing up to eternal life" (John 4:14).

When our inner well runs dry or becomes clogged with debris, Jesus invites us to rest beside him and to name the thirst that keeps us coming back again and again to be refreshed. Sitting beside the Well that is Christ, we receive the grace to discover that, created in the divine image, we have within us all we need to drink deep of eternal life. The author of the Gospel of John understands eternal life to mean life in all its fullness *now*.

A JOURNAL ENTRY: JANUARY 2002

The well is deep
fed by a living source
of clear, cold water,
which flows unceasingly.
To drink from that source
is to discover life and zesty, effervescent
joy.
Why do I choose
the dry, barren heat
in which to doze away
desire? "Come to the waters!"
The prophet's echo
reverberates from desert rock
and promises refreshment.
But I must rise and walk the dreary distance

leaving lethargy's
imprint on the sand.
The well is deep
but the Spring Source
has already drawn
the living water
and raises it to my lips.

SUGGESTIONS FOR REFLECTION

1. Read Isaiah 43:18-19. Do you sense that God is waiting to do something new in your life?

   Where do you notice wilderness places in your experience right now? How ready do you feel to leave behind old habits and patterns that clog your inner well? Ask God to enable you to perceive grace springing forth in your life.

2. Choose to spend some time by a water source—a river, well, pond, or the ocean—with no agenda other than being present with an open heart. Later you may wish to reflect on the experience by writing in your journal. What did you notice about your general mood, feelings, desires? How did your body respond to time beside the water?

3. Fill a glass bowl with water and place beside it a pile of rocks; either use small stones you have collected or purchase some

polished stones intended for water gardens. Place the bowl and rocks in a place where you will see them often during the day. Each time you become aware of some thought or action blocking your access to the living water, drop a stone in the bowl. At the end of the day, remove the stones with the awareness that they have been washed in the water. Allow each stone to become a prayer of gratitude and healing as you acknowledge your willingness to keep coming to the Source for strength to relinquish debris.

Chapter 7
Bread for the Journey

Jesus said to them, "I am the bread of life. Whoever comes to me will never be hungry."

—John 6:35

A small row house in Kildare, Ireland, is the destination of our pilgrimage group on a day filled with wind and rain. The city, known today for horse racing, is home to the Brigidine sisters mentioned earlier, who serve as peacemakers, gathering together Catholics and Protestants in celebration of the life and witness of Saint Brigid. Their small house is a place of gracious hospitality, and the doors open to welcome our group—pilgrims of several different denominations—into its cozy interior. We peel off our dripping coats and wet shoes and follow Sister Mary to a room just off the kitchen where a lantern throws light on a simple altar, its flame symbolizing the continuing witness of Brigid. We sit on chairs and cushions in this room, used as a chapel, first to drink steaming cups of hot tea, then to celebrate an ecumenical Eucharist.

Chapter Seven

We learn about the flame of Brigid, a saint whose compassion for God and for the poor and hungry often led her to give away her scarce supplies of food. Brigid has been called an "arrow of fire," since the fire of the Holy Spirit seemed to be with her at all times. Some said that they could see a flame above Brigid's head as she went about her ministry!

Sister Mary, a wonderful storyteller, relates that, for many centuries, the town seemed to have mostly forgotten the wisdom of their patron, Saint Brigid, who founded one of the great fifth-century Celtic double monasteries in the "church of the oak tree," Kildare. Today many pilgrims come to visit the (Anglican) parish church with its high tower and fire temple, Saint Brigid's well, and Solas Bhride, the sisters' home. Before we go out again into the rain-soaked town to visit these sites, we enjoy a feast of good things, including ample sandwiches, home-baked goods and, of course, more tea. The generosity of the sisters not only satisfies our hearty appetites but also feeds our soul's longing for Christ, the Bread of Life.

The pilgrim group stands together in the pit thought to be an ancient fire temple where a pre-Christian goddess, whose name also was Brigid, gathered her worshipers. During Celtic times every Christian monastery kept a fire burning constantly as a witness to the gospel; the place where we now stand was probably reclaimed as the site of Saint Brigid's fire. The high tower, a short distance away, was the place of security during times of attack, and some of us climb laboriously up seven sets of ladderlike steps. At the top, we are rewarded by a panoramic view of the city and lush green countryside beyond. At Saint Brigid's well, fed by an underground water source, we gather to pray our gratitude for this amazing woman who nurtured so many people, not only the monks and nuns of her monastery but also the many poor folk who came for sustenance. Because she was born out of wedlock, the child of a king and one of his slave women, Brigid suffered scorn but retained her unswerving faith in God.

Our Daily Bread

We walk through many wilderness places on the pilgrimage of our lives. Sometimes we feel empty, weary of moving day by day through arid terrain and hungry for the hope and joy with which we began the journey. Like our forebears in the journey of faith, we hope because God is faithful. "Hope is the simple trust that God has not forgotten the recipe for manna."[1] It is easy to be consumed by complaining self-pity and to see those who journey with us as encumbrances. Why does God no longer satisfy our longing for the bread of spiritual nurture and nourishing prayer? Why is this journey such a struggle and our family, friends, and church community so unsupportive? We mourn many losses in our lives, but we cannot find the comforting presence of Christ while we nostalgically long for the past.

This kind of fearful complaining was heard often among those who followed Moses out of Egypt: "The people complained in the hearing of the LORD about their misfortunes. . . . 'If only we had meat to eat! We remember the fish we used to eat in Egypt for nothing, the cucumbers, the melons, the leeks, the onions, and the garlic; but now our strength is dried up'" (Num. 11:1, 4-6). Moses bore the brunt of their complaining and resentment. In the daily struggle for survival and a new land in which to settle, the people forgot that they had left behind not only delicacies for which they yearned but also taskmasters and brickmaking under a fierce sun. When the spiritual journey is tough, we too may long for a past we see through rose-tinted spectacles!

When Jesus went into the desert to discern his call, the first temptation was to satisfy his craving for bread despite his commitment to a fast. Later, he would say to the disciples who, shocked when he welcomed a woman of doubtful reputation, urged him to eat: "I have food to eat that you do not know about. . . . My food is to do the will of him who sent me and to complete his work" (John 4:32, 34). On many occasions it must have been inconvenient for Jesus to respond to the needs of those who came for healing, and it must have been disappointing to find that even the disciples did not understand what he was talking about. No doubt Jesus was also sleep deprived as he responded to the overwhelming needs of others. Jesus was sustained in those times by his faithfulness to God through prayer, in both public synagogue worship and private prayer. He continued to do what he was called to do whether he felt rewarded or not. This was his food, the daily bread of single-minded obedience and trust in the One who had called him to a servant ministry.

Many years ago, my first spiritual director proved to be a wise guide who supported me through times of challenge. He often ended our session together with a simple imperative: "Go on!" Frequently this was not what I wanted to hear! I had spoken of my struggle to pray, the dullness of scripture, or other people who bumped up against me on the journey of faith. I wanted a formula for escaping the dry and difficult times. Perhaps I had read of a saint or contemporary follower of Christ whose experience made me hungry for the intimate relationship with God that this person seemed to have. Instead of encouraging me to emulate such individuals, my director would gently bring me back to my own life and circumstances with the words "Go on." This was wise counsel, especially in a culture that offers to assuage every human want with instant gratification. When the journey with God takes us through deserts, we are tempted to make detours and visit the smorgasbord of trendy spiritual delicacies to satisfy our appetite for fulfilling experiences.

To "go on" means consent to the everydayness of the journey, sustained by spiritual disciplines that provide a structure for growth during times of dryness or boredom. Like a trellis supporting plants in the garden, a sustained commitment to daily prayer and corporate worship gives structure and freedom. When we grow weary and hungry for a richer experience, we can learn to trust the framework instead of depending too readily on experiences of rapture or joy. The Greek word *hupomone* is one of the most frequently repeated in New Testament exhortations. The word may be translated as "steadfastness," "faithfulness," and sometimes "endurance."

A former archbishop of Canterbury urged participants in a retreat I attended in London to comb the Greek New Testament in order to pay attention to each occurrence of *hupomone*. "Ask yourselves what God is saying to you through these references," he said. "Many Christians fail to live into the regular, day-by-day faithfulness, into genuine discipleship."

Some years later, after the archbishop had retired, he came to speak at the church I served in New York City. When he discovered I was on the staff, he invited me to join him for tea. We met in the Palm Court of the Plaza Hotel for a very proper English tea—the kind of tea kept alive by the British for the sake of visitors who think it is what the English do at 4:00 PM each afternoon! Over the scones, wafer-thin sandwiches, shortbread, and cakes—accompanied by hot tea poured from a silver teapot—we talked about my decision to leave England and seek ordination in the Episcopal Church of the United States.

Unlike his successor, Archbishop Donald Coggan had fully supported the ordination of women, and I had talked with him in London before I "crossed the pond." Now I reminded him of the retreat day he had led and told him that his instruction to pray with each of the texts containing the word *hupomone* was so helpful for those of us who were impatiently looking for a feast of good things in scripture. Peering at me through his small gold-rimmed spectacles, he said: "Ah, but did you do it?" In all honesty I had to confess that I had started on the project, but boredom intervened. I needed to return to the task.

In a time of good, when it seems that God is close and providing sustenance, the psalmist euphorically invites others to "taste and see that the LORD is good" (Ps. 34:8). Once we have tasted the joy of God, we want it again and again, and we may be unwilling to eat the dry bread of faithfulness in the ordinary tasks of each day, including our prayer. The seventeenth-century monk Brother Lawrence of the Resurrection shared his distaste for kitchen duty in his little book

The Practice of the Presence of God. By allowing ordinary duties to be offered as prayer out of love for God, he practiced awareness of holy presence in such a way that the pots and pans were handled as if they were sacred altar vessels. Brother Lawrence did not consider worship with the community as "real" prayer and menial tasks as secondary; all was prayer and God was in all.

Brother Lawrence learned and lived the meaning of *hupomone*—the patient going on day by day without demanding instant gratification. He wrote to a mother superior who often asked for his counsel and enclosed a reply to a young sister filled with enthusiasm for God and her new life. He comments on the younger nun, saying: "She appears to me to be full of good will but she wants to go faster than grace."[2] No fast-food restaurants desecrate the landscape of prayer. And there are no instant recipes for escaping the hungers that challenge us when our journey takes us through difficult places; grace is given in the slow, dry areas. If we try to outrun it, we will become exhausted.

Hunger for "Soul Bread"

At the beginning of a thirty-day Ignatian retreat, my director handed me wise advice written by an earlier Jesuit, Pierre Teilhard de Chardin. I needed it often, especially when, sometimes for whole days, I prayed with no sense of joy and no experience of God's presence. This type of retreat removes many distractions that keep us from prayer, but our ingenious minds create others that insidiously beckon us to feed on their nutritionless fare. Aware of powerlessness over these diversions, it is easy to become disheartened and attempt

to outrun grace; I did that often. I still turn to Teilhard de Chardin
when impatience and weariness overcome me:

> Above all, trust in the slow work of God
> We are quite naturally impatient in everything
>   to reach the end without delay.
> We should like to skip the intermediate stages.
> We are impatient of being on the way to something
>   unknown, something new.
> And yet it is the law of progress
>   that it is made by passing through
>   some stages of instability—
>   and that it may take a very long time.
>
> And so I think it is with you.
>   your ideas mature gradually—let them grow,
>   let them shape themselves, without undue haste.
> Don't try to force them on,
>   as though you could be today what time
>   (that is to say, grace and circumstances
>   acting on your own good will)
>   will make of you tomorrow.
>
> Only God could say what this new spirit
>   gradually forming within you will be.
> Give Our Lord the benefit of believing
>   that his hand is leading you,
> and accept the anxiety of feeling yourself
>   in suspense and incomplete.[3]

King David knew that God does set a table for us in the wilderness through which we are led. There are also times when pastures are green and, resting beside still waters, our souls are restored, even when enemies remain (Ps. 23). Jesus, surrounded by a huge crowd hungry for his words of healing and hope, became aware that after long hours these people were physically hungry as well. The disciples wanted to bring down the curtain, send the people home, but Jesus said, "You give them something to eat" (Matt. 14:16). Impossible. They did not have the resources to satisfy such a large mob! The one who called himself the Bread of Life acted when a little bread and a few fish were offered to him; he blessed the food and had it distributed among the people; everyone had enough to eat. Some have suggested that the generosity of the small boy who offered his lunch to Jesus inspired others to unwrap hidden food and to share it with those who had none. How we interpret this story is less important than knowing that Jesus the Christ can satisfy all our hungers and calls upon us to feed those around us who are hungry in body, mind, and spirit.

At the end of John's Gospel we find a story about Peter, accompanied by some of the disciples, going fishing in the Sea of Galilee. After a long and fruitless night of fishing, a stranger near the shore calls out that they should try the other side of the boat. We can only imagine the irritation of experienced fishermen receiving advice from a stranger; probably their responses were not appropriate for recording in the Gospel! They do, however, try the other side of the boat. Miraculously, their nets fill to overflowing. John probably makes a connection with an earlier experience recorded in Luke, and he cried out, "It is the Lord!" (John 21:7). Peter hastily dresses, then jumps overboard in a flash, swimming and wading his way toward Jesus.

When they all get to shore and haul in the fish, Jesus has a fire ready with fish already cooking on it, but he tells the disciples to bring some of their catch. This suggests to me that, though Jesus had plenty to satisfy their hunger, he invited them to add the results of their labor to his abundance. God does set a table for us in the wilderness of loss, fear, doubt, boredom, disappointment, and impatience. That table is replenished by the gifts we offer one another. Listening to a depressed sister or brother, offering child care to an overwrought mother, giving time, produce from the garden, or a welcoming smile to a stranger—in these simple ways we assist God in setting the table. "You give them something to eat" (Matt. 14:16). "Bring some of the fish that you have just caught" (John 21:10). "I am the bread of life. Whoever comes to me will never be hungry, and whoever believes in me will never be thirsty" (John 6:35).

Let us come to the table with open hands and a willing heart. Let us come together as people of much faith and people of little faith. As the bread is broken and the wine shared, let us gratefully receive the gifts that sustain us in life, knowing that our brokenness is held in God's gentle hands to be blessed and given for the world.

A JOURNAL ENTRY: JULY 23, 2002

What joy and privilege! A bear comes to my yard to eat at the bird feeders and to teach me the wildness and fierce beauty of God. Her three little ones play, then climb a tree when I fearfully rattle the window. She stays!

Holy One, your unpredictability and wildness scare me;
your fierce beauty challenges me; but you are unshoo-
able! You do what you will, what you must, while I hide,
fearful, resisting vulnerability. I want to trust myself to
you, become a cub, play close to your maternal side, and
let you feed me from your abundance in times of desert
wandering. Thanks be that your love is untamed.

SUGGESTIONS FOR REFLECTION

1. Read Luke 24:13-35. Use your imagination to be present with the two disappointed travelers as they walk along the dusty road from Jerusalem to home. Become aware of the hope stirred by the stranger and of your desire to go on listening to him. As you enter the house and he sits with you at the table, allow yourself to experience the joy of recognition. Consider times when Christ has walked with you, but you did not recognize him.

2. Write your own psalm to celebrate the times that God has set a table for you in wilderness times. Psalm 23 might be used as a template for your own psalm.

3. Ponder the following invitation God gave to Laodicean Christians: "Listen! I am standing at the door, knocking; if you hear my voice and open the door, I will come in to you and eat with you, and you with me" (Rev. 3:20). Do you hear Christ

knocking, humbly waiting to be invited into your soul home? What keeps you from inviting him inside? What might you set before him so that you may feast together?

Chapter 8

Homecoming

In my Father's house there are many dwelling places.

—John 14:2

Sweet-smelling honeysuckle fills the hedgerows; sheep graze on hillsides made green by early spring rains. A journey through the Welsh countryside brings our pilgrim group to the small village of Pennant Melangell (pronounced Mellanangeth) where we must leave our bus to walk the narrow pilgrim way to the church of Saint Melangell. We do not speak as we journey but pray for God's grace that our hearts, ears, and eyes may be open to the blessing of this time and place. Scented air, immature hazelnuts growing abundantly, a blue sky, sheep and crows breaking the silence, and our own footsteps crunching on the gravel surface of the road—all become part of of this journey. As we near the end of the road and the small rock-built church comes into view, we see a figure wearing a black cassock waiting to greet each pilgrim and welcome us to this place she calls home. The Reverend Margaret Davies has lived in Pennant Melangell for many years, first as the schoolteacher wife of the Church of Wales priest and, since his death and her own ordination, as a priest in her own right. Her welcoming smile is contagious.

Some members of our group are a little footsore, and the unusually warm weather prompts extra gratitude as we enter the cool church. This church houses the twelfth-century CE shrine of the saint who has been honored in these hills for fourteen hundred years. We listen eagerly to her story, told by Margaret. Melangell was a young woman who came from Ireland in about 600 CE seeking a place of solitude and prayer. When she arrived in this valley, she recognized it as her "desert" and place of resurrection. It was not too long before other women joined her, and Pennant Melangell became the center of a large community of sisters. Like so many other Celtic saints, Melangell had a close connection with animals. One day a local prince came to hunt in the valley with his horses and dogs, who flushed a terrified hare from the fields. Though young and defenseless, Melangell protected the hare beneath the folds of her cloak, refusing to release it to the snarling dogs and impressing the prince by her courage. It is said that after he gave the valley to Melangell and her community, it became a place of healing and hope for many in need of compassion.

The ministry of healing continues, not only through regular daily worship at the church but also through the work of the center built to welcome pilgrims, the sick, and the needy who come for respite. Margaret and her assistant invite us for lunch, lovingly prepared and home-baked at the center. A small gate set in a whitewashed stone wall leads into a beautiful, flower-filled garden with many places to sit quietly. A gentle fountain adds to the sense of peacefulness. The grounds and house are wheelchair-accessible, and we learn that terminally ill patients are brought here to sit for a few hours where fragrant air, loving attention, and prayer are offered. Many of those who come live in the tenements of Liverpool or other large cities. They spend their days housebound, suffering from lack of quality nursing care and few visitors. Here Saint Melangell's influence continues as the sick are healed, the dying comforted, and pilgrims receive gracious welcome.

Our visit ends with a Eucharist, celebrated in the ancient church and attended by some of the regular worshipers. In the tower of the church a photographic display depicts the restoration process begun during the life of Margaret's husband. Charles, Prince of Wales, appears often in the pictures. Visits are not publicly announced, but Prince Charles chooses this remote spot as a place of quiet rest and spiritual renewal. I can understand why.

When her husband died after a battle with cancer, Margaret committed herself to a continuation of the healing work already begun in Pennant Melangell. She was a deacon in the Church of Wales and approached the bishop to request ordination as soon as women were permitted to become priests. The bishop gladly agreed to ordain her and appointed her pastor to replace her spouse. She also developed cancer and now shares her experience of God's healing grace with others who face life-threatening illness.

On the night before we arrived, a shepherd out on the hills suffered a severe heart attack; Margaret was called to his side. Clearly he was dying; he had no wish to be transported to the nearest hospital, and in any case it would take a long time for an ambulance to navigate the narrow lanes. He lay in the field, surrounded by his flock, and Margaret stayed with him, cradling his head in her arms as a soft wind blew around them. It was a beautiful death, she told us. A star-studded sky overhead and sheep bleating in the hills where the farmer had spent his entire life was his "place of resurrection." This term was used by the Celtic Christians who traveled with the Spirit and intuitively knew that the place where they settled was the place from which they would depart to live more fully when death conveyed them to life with the risen Christ.

Celtic Christians viewed death as resurrection and homecoming. The fear and pretense prevailing today in funeral homes, where those we love are so often robbed of their natural appearance in death, are challenged by our Celtic forebears. I have not attended an Irish wake, but I understand that, though participants do not deny their loss (accompanied by a good deal of wailing), they also have a party. Families and friends gather around the body of the loved one, sometimes laid out on a kitchen table. They relate their memories and tell stories about the deceased, their tales laced with lavish quantities of the local brew. The Celtic mind does not totally separate this world and the world where resurrection life is experienced in its fullness. Celtic tradition recognizes many "thin" places where the membrane between earth and heaven is almost permeable. Pennant Melangell is certainly one of them.

Heading for Home

On the life journey we undertake as God's people, we do not wander aimlessly but walk with and toward the Holy One. Sometimes we may feel lost along the way, but always the divine Presence travels with us. When the Hebrew people moved through the trackless deserts seeking a homeland, God's presence was represented in "a pillar of cloud by day, to lead them along the way, and in a pillar of fire by night" (Exod. 13:21). The "Shekinah" glory of God, revealed in the brightness of cloud, was manifested to God's people on many occasions. When the Hebrews complained about lack of food and Moses interceded for them, the Shekinah appeared; on Mount Sinai, when the law was handed down to their leader, the people again saw the cloud. Moses had first experienced God's awesome presence in the fire that failed to consume a bush in the desert, thus cloud and fire became primary symbols of the awesomeness of God, who always urged the people onward.

Jesus, preparing his disciples for his death and resurrection, told them it was to their advantage that he "go away," a statement that seemed contradictory. How could they possibly be better off without him? Confusion reigned among the disciples. They wanted to ask many questions of their Master, who had embarrassed them by stooping to wash their feet. Jesus reassured them: "In my Father's house there are many dwelling places. . . . And if I go and prepare a place for you, I will come again and will take you to myself, so that where I am, there you may be also" (John 14:2-3).

Thomas wanted to know how they would find the way. In one of his many I AM statements, which echo the name God gave to Moses, Jesus replied, "I am the way." Still confused, the disciples asked for more reassurance and learned that "another Advocate" would come alongside them to continue the earthly ministry of Jesus. The word that John uses for the Spirit in this section of the Gospel has been translated in many ways: Advocate, Counselor, Comforter, and sometimes, in transliteration, as Paraclete. By using this word, Jesus implies that the Spirit will be for them the same as Jesus has been. The Spirit will show disciples the way as God's Shekinah presence led the children of Israel in the wilderness.

When Luke describes the Day of Pentecost, he uses the images of fire and wind to communicate the life-changing fulfillment of Jesus' promise of the Spirit. The followers of Jesus could now continue on the Way, empowered by the awe-inspiring phenomenon of the Christ presence, manifested through symbols that had represented God throughout the Hebrew scriptures—fire, wind, and cloud. Those followers who had fearfully gone into hiding, meeting only behind locked doors, are transformed by their experience in the upper room and are soon out among the people sharing the good news. Peter, who had been living with the shame of denying Jesus, now preaches boldly that the Hebrew scriptures had predicted this day in Joel 2:28:

> In the last days it will be, God declares,
> that I will pour out my Spirit upon all flesh,
>   and your sons and your daughters shall prophesy,
> and your young men shall see visions,
>   and your old men shall dream dreams. (Acts 2:17)

Peter announces to the crowd that Joel's words have been fulfilled in the person of Jesus of Nazareth, the man who did many signs among the people and then was crucified. "But God raised him up, having freed him from death, because it was impossible for him to be held in its power" (Acts 2:24). In this Jesus, death has been conquered and new life becomes available to all.

The Spirit of God, who breathed over the waters in the Creation story of Genesis 1, was the same Spirit who came upon individuals to enable them to fulfill tasks to which God had called them. In the life of Elijah, the Spirit was clearly evident. When his successor, Elisha, prepared to take over his master's work, he asked, "Please let me inherit a double share of your spirit" (2 Kings 2:9). The Day of Pentecost dramatically demonstrated that the Spirit was no longer present only to specially anointed servants of God. From that day on, the Spirit of God became available to every person willing to call upon the name of Jesus Christ, crucified, risen, ascended, and alive in the world. Death no longer held terror for those who believed in Christ and trusted his promise to prepare a dwelling place for them in his Father's house.

The writer of the letter to the Hebrews represents Christian life as a journey. The letter invites us to reflect on the forebears in the faith whose stories inspire our own. He uses many images from the Old Testament to portray the Christian way, and, just as the ancient Hebrews regarded Jerusalem and the Temple on Mount Zion as their true home, so followers of Christ travel toward the new Zion of heaven. The Christian community provides a supportive "home" while we are on earth, but it is important to remember that "here we have no lasting city, but we are looking for the city that is to come" (Heb. 13:14). Christ, through the power of the Holy Spirit, leads us into fullness of life as we follow him on earth, yet an even greater fullness awaits us beyond the grave.

Celtic Christians tell many stories of the death of saints in their time, describing the transition from embodiment to life beyond human form in terms of glory, peace, hope, and openhearted joy.

Chapter Eight

One of the many prayers collected from the Highlands and islands of Scotland during the closing years of the nineteenth century by Alexander Carmichael offers insight into the Celtic Christian understanding of death:

> Thou goest home this night to thy home of winter,
> To thy home of autumn, of spring, and of summer;
> Thou goest home this night to thy perpetual home,
> To thine eternal bed, to thine eternal slumber.
> . . . .
> Sleep, O sleep in the calm of all calm,
> Sleep, O sleep in the guidance of guidance,
> Sleep, O sleep in the love of all loves;
> Sleep, O beloved, in the Lord of life,
> Sleep, O beloved, in the God of life![1]

God is the journey and the homecoming. God accompanies us through deserts and mountains, through struggle and rest, in the company of those we love and those who challenge us. At times we become disillusioned, tired, and fearful, but in the darkest moments, we discover a table in the wilderness to sustain our souls. God has provided us with many stories to help us along the way. Stories of hope, fidelity, and victory abound, but also we find stories in which we learn that failure is never final in the divine economy. The Lover of our souls meets us at every stopping place, yet teaches us that God's home is also within us and that one day we will sit together at the great feast of ultimate life and joy.

A Journal Entry: April 10, 1992

I sit outside in the cool of the morning; no mosquitoes are awake yet! Gratitude for my new home fills me, and I find I am beginning to be more at home in these mountains and in myself.

Thank you, Holy One.

Suggestions for Reflection

1. Read Hebrews 12:1-2. Whom do you count among the great "cloud of witnesses" who have supported you on your journey? How do you understand *homecoming* from this passage?

2. In the first chapter of John's Gospel, some disciples of John the Baptist begin to follow Jesus. When he stops and asks them, "What are you looking for?" They reply, "Where are you staying?" Jesus gives the invitation "Come and see!" These disciples spend time at home with Jesus, and after their conversation, they set out on a new path to follow him. Begin a dialogue with Christ in your journal. Allow him to ask, "What are you looking for?" Respond honestly, and as the dialogue continues, notice your changing emotions, desires, and any blocks that keep you from being at home with Christ. Allow the conversation to be expressed in prayer and listen for the responses Christ makes.

Note: This may sound like a contrived way of entering into

conversation with Christ, but it can become a powerful means of discerning where you are and what you need or long for.

3. Invite someone into your home for a meal. As you sit at table with your guest, notice how you see Christ in that individual.

Group Leader's Guide

The structure of this book allows for both individual and group use. The following suggestions will help group leaders design and facilitate meetings. Established groups, such as covenant or Bible study groups, may wish to continue established patterns for meetings but may find valuable suggestions here for sharing insights. If several members in a group are experienced leaders, consider rotating facilitation of each gathering.

Getting Started

Decide on the number and dates of meetings for group study. Eight meeting times and an additional review or retreat session are recommended. If a new group is being formed, an introductory session to outline the content, format, and expectations of participants—with no obligation to join—will reduce the dropout rate that can result from unclear information about commitment. Details of dates, time, and space for meeting should be communicated clearly.

For a large group, plan to divide into breakout groups for sharing. The ideal number for the small groups is six to eight persons. Each small group needs a leader.

Invitation and Promotions

A brochure or flyer with details about the series and specific information about contact person(s) for those who want more information will foster interest and commitment. State a deadline for signing up because the numbers will determine the structure of meetings. If the group is to be formed from within a congregation, the organizer may request an opportunity to outline the intention and value of the series during a worship gathering.

Stress the importance of participants' presence at all sessions. Also note that additional participants will not be invited to join after the first week. These understandings will ensure the integrity of the group(s) and the environment to build trust.

Hospitality

Be aware of the space in which you will meet and make it as hospitable as possible. An ugly room can be transformed by color and plants. Create an altar: a table, covered with a cloth holding plants, a candle, and other objects of beauty. Participants may contribute by bringing items of importance to them in their spiritual journey and adding them to the centerpiece.

If you intend to serve beverages or snacks at the sessions, plan to do that outside the meeting room if possible. Encourage people to enter the meeting space quietly rather than chitchat over coffee there.

You may set up a registration table with name tags outside the room on the first evening. Designate someone to greet participants and offer additional information. This table could be used at subsequent meetings for reminders, relevant brochures, books, and items members of the group would like to share with one another.

Remember to order books well in advance of the gatherings and decide whether you will make these available before the study begins or on the first evening. Since journaling will be an important activity, either make sure that participants bring journals or plan to provide them with blank notebooks to be used throughout the series. Supply pens, pencils, and paper.

Unless you are constrained by time, include a creative activity at each meeting and have art and other appropriate supplies available. You will need a CD or tape player and recordings of reflective music to use as people enter the room and during some of the meditations.

Session Structure

An ideal time frame for group sessions is one and a half to two hours, which will enable participants to enter deeply into the material and to incorporate creativity into their prayer. The following is a suggested structure for each meeting:

- *Gathering, opening prayer, and sharing.* After the first week, group members share their reflections on the chapter read and journal writing. If the group is large, the initial gathering and prayer may be brief. Include the scripture reading for the book chapter studied over the previous week and the meditation/reflection exercise. Invite the participants to move in silence to their smaller groups.

- *Meditation/reflection exercise.* At this time participants may be introduced to a variety of models for prayer: guided meditation, scripture reflection using active imagination, body prayer, chant, "seeing" prayer with an icon, prayer with a natural object such as a leaf, praying with clay or art materials.

- *Break (or move into small groups).*

- *Small group* lectio divina *(see p. 125) exercise.* Use the scripture passage suggested for the next chapter of the book. This initial response to the passage—how it touches each person's life today— can set the scene for further journal writing and reflection in the coming days.

- *Closing worship.*

A small group with time constraints might begin with an opening prayer/meditation followed by a short silence. Someone may read the passage suggested for reflection—or choose a different scripture on the theme—and then invite each person to share insights. Encourage "I" statements and explain that first the participants will *listen* to one another before discussion begins. The leader can model this sharing style, including brevity when speaking. You might pass a rock—the group's "wilderness rock"—from hand to hand as a sacred recognition that the person holding the rock is to be honored by attentiveness, not conversation.

At the end of the gathering, make sure everyone understands the next assignment before closing with a brief worship activity and prayer.

Retreat

If at all possible, plan a longer gathering at the end of the eight study sessions—an experience of unhurried time with God. You may wish to engage group members in thinking about a retreat day, and it may be appropriate to invite your clergyperson to celebrate Eucharist and bless the members of the group as they continue their journey of faith. Marking a point of closure is important even if the group chooses to continue in some form. It may well be that leaders emerge from this first gathering and begin to facilitate other groups.

Group *Lectio Divina*

This model for reflecting on scripture is sometimes called the African Model. Its design helps each person to reflect on scripture, not so much to understand and study the writings as to allow them to "speak" to the present moment. The focus on listening and brief responses makes it suitable for people of diverse ages, faith traditions, and knowledge of the Bible.

1. Begin with a few moments of silent prayer.

2. Ask one person to read the selected passage slowly.

3. Ask participants to name silently a word or phrase that caught their attention (one minute).

4. Invite each member to share the word or phrase with the group. The leader can model this by sharing his or her word first without explanation, elaboration, or discussion.

5. Ask another group member to read the passage again.

6. Invite participants to silently name and/or write down their awareness of where the scripture touches their lives today (three to five minutes).

7. Ask each person to share his or her reflection, beginning with "I" statements. Remind group members that this is not a discussion session. They are simply to listen attentively.

8. Invite a third person to read the scripture.

9. This time the group silently names or writes down a response to the question: *What does God want me to do or be this week? Is God asking me to change in any way?*

10. Again share around the group, using "I" statements.

11. To close, all stand and join hands. Each participant prays for the person on his or her right (leader begins). Explain that people may pray silently or aloud. Their prayers embody what their neighbor has said in the group. If the prayer is silent, a hand-squeeze signals the next person when the prayer has been offered. Then that person prays for the next individual in the circle.

Notes

CHAPTER ONE

1. Athanasius, *Life of Saint Antony* (Red Sea, Egypt: St. Antony's Monastery, n.d.), 46.

2. John Moses, *The Desert: An Anthology for Lent* (Harrisburg, Pa.: Morehouse Publishing, 1997), 16.

3. Thomas Merton, *Thoughts in Solitude* (New York: Farrar, Straus, and Giroux, 1958), 119.

CHAPTER TWO

1. During their long wandering in the wilderness, the people grumbled, remembering nostalgically food that they now lacked: "The rabble among them had a strong craving. . . . 'We remember the fish we used to eat in Egypt for nothing, the cucumbers, the melons, the leeks, the onions, and the garlic; but now our strength is dried up, and there is nothing at all but this manna to look at'" (Num. 11:4-6).

2. Edward C. Sellner, *Wisdom of the Celtic Saints* (Notre Dame, Ind.: Ave Maria Press, 1993), 60.

3. Macrina Wiederkehr, *Seasons of Your Heart: Prayers and Reflections*, rev. ed. (San Francisco: HarperSanFrancisco, 1991), 185.

CHAPTER FOUR

1. The Book of Common Prayer (New York: Oxford University Press, 1990), 112.

CHAPTER FIVE

1. Some of the references to John O'Donohue come from a conference he led in Asheville, North Carolina, in November 2001. His books explore the wisdom of Celtic spirituality and offer poetic images and prayers that inspire hope for contemporary seekers. His books include *Anam Cara: A Book of Celtic Wisdom*, *Eternal Echoes: Celtic Reflections on Our Yearning to Belong*, and *Conamara Blues: Poems*, all published by Cliff Street Books, an imprint of HarperCollins, New York.

2. Alexander Carmichael, *Carmina Gadelica*, ed. C. J. Moore, rev. ed. (Edinburgh: Floris Books, 1992), 248.

CHAPTER SEVEN

1. W. Paul Jones, *Trumpet at Full Moon: An Introduction to Christian Spirituality as Diverse Practice* (Louisville, Ky.: Westminster/John Knox Press, 1992), 84.

2. Brother Lawrence of the Resurrection, *The Practice of the Presence of God*, trans. John J. Delaney (New York: Image Books, 1977), 78.

3. "Patient Trust" by Pierre Teilhard de Chardin in *Hearts on Fire: Praying with Jesuits*, ed. Michael Harter (St. Louis, Mo.: The Institute of Jesuit Sources, 1993), 58.

CHAPTER EIGHT

1. Carmichael, *Carmina Gadelica*, 312–13.

About the Author

ELIZABETH CANHAM is a priest in the Episcopal Church who offers a ministry of teaching and spiritual formation in an ecumenical context. She grew up in England, taught in a British seminary, and has served parishes in London, New Jersey, New York, and Western North Carolina. For five years she directed retreat ministry at Holy Savior Priory in South Carolina. Dr. Canham founded Stillpoint Ministries in 1992 to offer spirituality conferences, group and individual guidance, and retreats. Stillpoint and its resources were gladly given to a larger organization in 2002.

Since 1976 Dr. Canham has led many pilgrimages, including visits to Israel, Egypt, Europe, and Celtic sites in the British Isles. She continues her ministry through Hospites Mundi, offering her services to churches and other organizations as speaker, leader, and consultant.

Earlier books include *Heart Whispers: Benedictine Wisdom for Today* from Upper Room Books, as well as *Pilgrimage to Priesthood; Praying the Bible,* and *Journaling with Jeremiah.* Dr. Canham has contributed to *Christian Century, Weavings,* and *Episcopal Life.* She lives in the North Carolina mountains with two Celtic cats—Bede and Brigid.

Other titles of Interest
from
Upper Room Books

Calming the Restless Spirit: A Journey Toward God by Ben Campbell Johnson ISBN 0-8358-0814-9

Enter by the Gate: Jesus' 7 Guidelines When Making Hard Choices Flora Slosson Wuellner ISBN 0-8358-9883-0

Heart Whispers: Benedictine Wisdom for Today by Elizabeth J. Canham ISBN 0-8358-0892-0

Jesus, Our ndy
J. Miller

Travelin
9857-1

A Wake ll
Jenkins

Wrestlin fe
Robert